Donald Juda
1977

THE NETHERLANDS

(Frontispiece, overleaf): A house front in Leeuwarden

Sacheverell Sitwell

THE
NETHERLANDS

Photographs by Cas Oorthuys

B. T. Batsford Ltd
London

First published 1974
Copyright © Sacheverell Sitwell 1974

ISBN 0 7134 2779 5

Made and printed in Great Britain by
Cox & Wyman Ltd, London, Fakenham and Reading
for the publishers, B. T. Batsford Ltd,
4 Fitzhardinge Street, London W1

Contents

Acknowledgments

Every endeavour has been made to keep this new edition of *The Netherlands* up-to-date after the lapse of years since 1948 when it first appeared. The author undertook a special journey to Holland in April, 1973, for this purpose. He would like to thank Councillor Miss A. Stenfert-Kroese of the Embassy of The Netherlands in London, and the Ministry of Foreign Affairs of The Netherlands in The Hague for granting him facilities. He journeyed from end to end of Holland covering some 600 miles. And here again he would like to thank Mrs Louise van Everdingen who was put in charge of us and accompanied us throughout. We were able to see the Royal Château of Het Loo, and thank Baron van Hasbeck, its curator, for our visit. Its restoration is a sign of the growing interest in Daniel Marot. The author would like to express his gratitude to Miss S. Dorr of The Netherlands Foreign Office; to Miss Etka Schrijver of Amsterdam for her encyclopaedic knowledge and enthusiasm; and to Miss Sytse Engelsma of the Frisian Museum in Leeuwarden. Not the least delight of the journey was to visit Friesland again; while the final chapter on Zeeland has been entirely re-written, and was the crowning pleasure of this undertaking.

The Author and Publisher would like to thank Cas Oorthuys of Amsterdam for permission to use all the photographs appearing in this book. The map is by kind permission of Patrick Leeson.

List of Illustrations

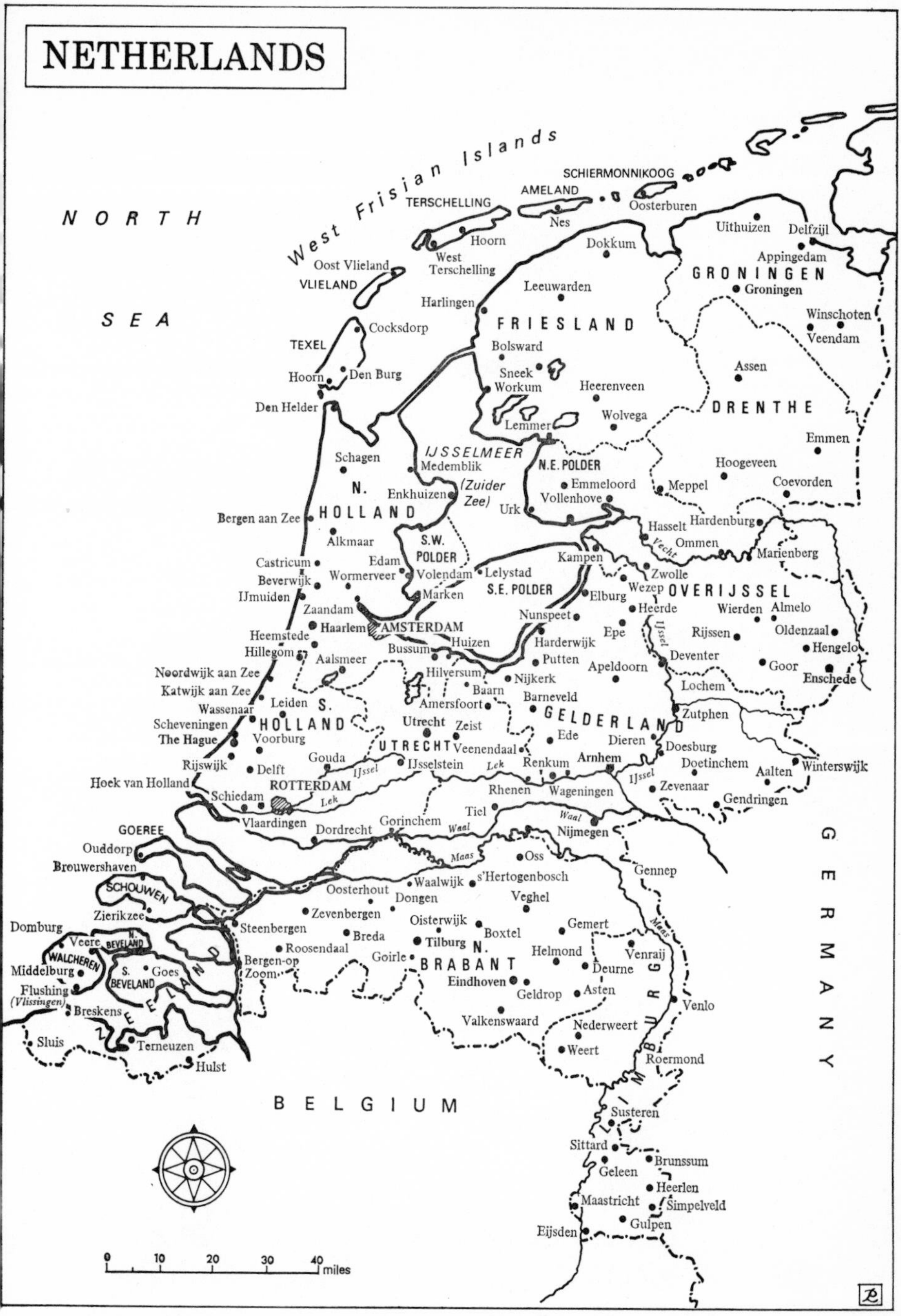

NETHERLANDS
NORTH
SEA
West Frisian Islands
TERSCHELLING
AMELAND
SCHIERMONNIKOOG
VLIELAND
TEXEL
GRONINGEN
FRIESLAND
DRENTHE
N.E. POLDER
IJSSELMEER
(Zuider Zee)
N. HOLLAND
S.W. POLDER
S.E. POLDER
OVERIJSSEL
GELDERLAND
S. HOLLAND
UTRECHT
N. BRABANT
ZEELAND
LIMBURG
GOEREE
SCHOUWEN
N. BEVELAND
S. BEVELAND
WALCHEREN
BELGIUM
GERMANY
Oosterburen
Nes
Hoorn
West Terschelling
Oost Vlieland
Harlingen
Cocksdorp
Den Burg
Hoorn
Den Helder
Dokkum
Leeuwarden
Uithuizen
Delfzijl
Appingedam
Groningen
Winschoten
Veendam
Bolsward
Sneek
Workum
Heerenveen
Wolvega
Lemmer
Assen
Emmen
Schagen
Medemblik
Enkhuizen
Urk
Emmeloord
Vollenhove
Meppel
Hoogeveen
Coevorden
Bergen aan Zee
Alkmaar
Castricum
Beverwijk
IJmuiden
Edam
Wormerveer
Volendam
Marken
Lelystad
Kampen
Hasselt
Hardenburg
Ommen
Marienberg
Vecht
Zwolle
Wezep
Heerde
Elburg
Zaandam
Haarlem
AMSTERDAM
Heemstede
Hillegom
Aalsmeer
Bussum
Huizen
Nunspeet
Harderwijk
Epe
Wierden
Almelo
Rijssen
Oldenzaal
Hengelo
Enschede
Goor
Deventer
IJssel
Putten
Apeldoorn
Nijkerk
Hilversum
Baarn
Amersfoort
Barneveld
Lochem
Zutphen
Noordwijk aan Zee
Katwijk aan Zee
Wassenaar
Leiden
Scheveningen
The Hague
Voorburg
Rijswijk
Delft
Gouda
IJssel
IJsselstein
Utrecht
Zeist
Veenendaal
Ede
Dieren
Doesburg
Doetinchem
Aalten
Winterswijk
Renkum
Arnhem
Lek
Rhenen
Wageningen
Zevenaar
Gendringen
Hoek van Holland
Schiedam
ROTTERDAM
Lek
Vlaardingen
Dordrecht
Gorinchem
Waal
Tiel
Waal
Nijmegen
Ouddorp
Brouwershaven
Maas
Oss
Gennep
Oosterhout
Waalwijk
s'Hertogenbosch
Dongen
Veghel
Zierikzee
Zevenbergen
Steenbergen
Breda
Oisterwijk
Boxtel
Tilburg
Gemert
Domburg
Veere
Roosendaal
Bergen-op Zoom
Goirle
Helmond
Venraij
Deurne
Middelburg
Goes
Eindhoven
Geldrop
Asten
Flushing
(Vlissingen)
Breskens
Valkenswaard
Venlo
Nederweert
Sluis
Terneuzen
Hulst
Weert
Roermond
Susteren
Sittard
Brunssum
Geleen
Heerlen
Maastricht
Simpelveld
Gulpen
Eijsden
0
10
20
30
40
miles

1. Introduction

Upon a map of the world The Netherlands are but a little speck, an estuary and a chain or two of islands. The part they have played in history is out of all proportion to their size. They founded a fabulous empire at the far side of the world, in the remote East Indies, with a native population of some 60 millions. They have possessions in the West Indies, and only failed to retain dominion in North Atlantic America, in Brazil, at The Cape, and in Ceylon. It may be that the Dutch genius is more lasting than her colonies. As a race of artists they are second only to the Italians, while they have shown repeatedly, and lately, that they possess qualities which are lacking to the mercurial South. Their arts are now dormant in this unpropitious time. It may be that the Dutch language is spoken by too few persons to afford great writers. Their talent in painting and in architecture will, more certainly, be born again, for it must be endemic in them, as poetry among the English.

The history and achievement of Europe have something missing if the Dutch are not included. But the definition of that quality is not easy to assess. Perhaps, more than all else, it is their sanity and mental balance, a natural law which is contradicted, as is the case, always, by the supreme genius of Rembrandt. Not that the bohemian temperament was lacking in their painters. If we think of Dutch painting, and it is the most famous of their products, we discover their peculiar merit to be that of persevering with a subject to the very end. That, and their improbable degree of sensibility in so stalwart and robust a race. This is even borne out in the fantasy of their local costumes, which for far-fetched imagination, for headdresses shaped like scallop shells, of straw, and lined with Indian chintzes, for painted ribbons and floating streamers, rival with the birds of paradise. The stolid Dutchman, we might say, would be the last person in the world to think of these. But, also, to paint Vermeer's *Lady at the Virginals,* or 100, or 1,000, other paintings. Their national genius would seem to consist in a mingling of poetry with prosaic fact. They are not to be separated from the sea, which is their medium and means of livelihood, and upon which the heroes of their race have triumphed, and upon occasion perished. But this book treats of the Dutch in peace, and not in war; our intention is to celebrate the man-made wonders of a largely artificial land, and with this excuse we launch it forth upon the canals and inland waters.

2. Dutch Water Towns

At the mention of Holland many persons will see an immediate picture in their minds, a convention or set piece not having, as we shall discover, more than a supernumerary resemblance to the truth. So much, or but little more, had been our own experience upon three or four visits of a few days only to The Netherlands. It has needed a deeper and more protracted study for what we believe to be a true portrait to emerge before our eyes. But while we mix the colours it would be well to enquire if an authentic image is not to be discerned even in the old traditional picture of the Dutchman or Hollander in his reclaimed land below the level of the waters. What we need for this purpose could be called a historical estimate of the Lowlanders. That is quickly accomplished, and it will leave us with a notion of importance, naval and mercantile, out of all proportion to the number of the population.

In the latter part of the sixteenth and the seventeenth centuries for we must accord the Dutch the compliment of considering them in their golden age, this is the state or chart of the world. The Venetians and Turks, both in decline, are the great powers of the Mediterranean. There remain the Spaniards, the French, the English, and the Dutch. Prussia is not yet a danger. Spain is the great military power in Europe. But the Dutch in pursuit of their freedom have challenged the Spaniards and after appalling struggles, protracted through the lives of two generations, have defeated them and forced them to withdraw from Holland. Later, and in their time, the Dutch have won victories over France and England. This is the day of Tromp and de Ruyter, the naval heroes of the Hollanders, and during and despite interminable wars, this race has become the richest nation in the world.

The great explorers are now Dutch and no longer Spaniards or Portuguese. The Dutch East India Company is established. Australia, Tasmania, New Zealand, owe their names to Dutchmen. Batavia is founded; and there are Dutch colonies in Ceylon, in Brazil, at The Cape of Good Hope, and at New Amsterdam or Manhattan on the Hudson River. In the beginning, from 1598, there had been no fewer than nine companies for traffic with the Near East and the Indies. It was 'privateering', as that has not been practised since the Greek cities founded their colonies along the littoral of the Mediterranean and Black Sea. The separate states, Zeeland for an example, might have their own trading companies, but in the end all were combined into one great corporation with headquarters, first in the Moluccas and then in Java. The Dutch, also, obtained the monopoly of all trade with Japan, under conditions so curious that they deserve separate treatment. About the same time the Dutch West India Company was set up with its chief factory at Manhattan, a venture that soon failed, but in our account of Friesland, more especially, we shall endeavour to prove that the little bands of Dissenters, Anabaptists, Mennonites, who sailed from Holland for North America, brought with them a culture that is alive today and that provides one of the more promising anachronisms of the United States. From the East Indies, for our purposes, the stream of influence flowed the other way. Certain Dutch villages upon the Zuyder Zee, owing to their isolation and remoteness, but whose menfolk were fishermen and mariners voyaging in the summer as far as Norway and buying chintzes and Indian stuffs for their women from the East India Company's magazines at Amsterdam and other ports, passed their lives in what was tantamount to a Celestial opium dream, evolving for themselves a fantastic semi- or mock-Indian costume regulated by Draconian rules of age and mourning, and a peculiar style of painted furniture. Their history and inhabitants form an aesthetic and psychological puzzle of the first importance.

The Dutch ships went forth upon the seas and brought back the

2   *The Baroque organ of St Bavo, Haarlem*

3 *Zaamo*

wealth of the Orient, and within a few years the 'Sea Beggars' had become the rich men of Europe. They and their ancestors had reclaimed their land, foot by foot, with as much effort as they pushed back the Spaniards. The dykes, like as many fortifications, must be kept perpetually in order. Perhaps the deliberate pace of the canals influenced the phlegmatic character of the Dutchmen. Amsterdam in the meantime had become a wealthier and more solemn Venice. For the pride of the Dutchmen was their cities, and they welcomed to them all persons fleeing from religious persecution. The material prosperity of the Dutch at home is enhanced or illustrated, which way we look at it, by the presence of philosophers, Descartes and Spinoza, and many men of science. Dutch literature of the golden epoch the foreigner must leave, perforce, unopened and with uncut pages. Vondel, we are told, was contemporary, or was he more than that, to Milton? But there are Rembrandt, Frans Hals, and the unending host of minor painters. The painters of Holland are her present renown, now that her merchants and counting houses are no longer foremost. It is, indeed, this multiplicity of paintings that colours the picture of Holland and closes the calendar of her history before the seventeenth century has reached its end. There is even evidence that the painting of pictures had become a craze like that for tulip growing. Holland has too many painters. Rembrandt and Frans Hals, like great artists in other lands, are suffered to die, bankrupt and in misery, while, below them, such is the plethora of names and details that the foreigner, perhaps also the Dutchman, is likely to visit the Rijksmuseum or the Mauritshuis and come away bewildered.

The race of Hollanders, small in numbers, has left the strongest visual evidence upon a changing world. Physically, even spiritually, they are nearer to the English than any other nation. Or are they more nearly related in some ways to a part of the population of the United States? This we can say : there may be ties of sympathy in many other respects, but racially daemonically, Calais Pier is 100 times more remote from our shores than The Hook of Holland. And the Dutch are so much nearer to us than the Germans. They are like the Scots and English, but without the Welsh or Irish. Perhaps the main difference is that they have no Norman blood. But the racial resemblance or affinity between the two peoples reaches its complete expression in the red brick architecture. In Holland this is conditioned, not by streets but by canals. This affected the planning of Dutch houses; but transferred to England, and altered, the brick architecture is in so many ways more suited to us than the chill Palladian from Italy. Beautiful little buildings of modest proportions from the seventeenth and eighteenth centuries are to be found in so many towns in Holland. Those of earlier date are rare, and more often smaller still, bearing witness to how modest were the Dutch resources till the East India trade began. Of Dutch architecture there is an immense, an even preponderant body of buildings not yet, we believe, appreciated by the Dutch themselves. As for the later houses of Amsterdam they resemble very nearly their counterparts in London, but, within, they are a riot of stucco, while several have painted rooms which even an enthusiast for the Rococo would not anticipate from outside. We will speak of these presently, as of the three or four astonishing interiors by Daniel Marot in old houses at The Hague. None, so far as we know, has yet been mentioned or illustrated in any work written in the English language. This was decidedly the case when the first edition of this book came out in 1948, and but little has been written about it since then, for which reason the 'Dutch' number of the magazine *Apollo* for November 1972 is doubly welcome. In general, we may say that the typical gabled houses of Holland have no lack of admirers, but that the later houses of the eighteenth century are no less models of inward exuberance and exterior restraint.

Let us take an instance. Pertaining to the period, or a little earlier, it may be enquired where more glorious buildings are to be seen than the private houses upon either bank of the Rapenburg, or grand canal of Leyden, not palaces, but houses belonging to learned doctors of the University, or rich burghers? Leyden was during the seventeenth century the most famous school of medicine in Europe, at a time when medicine was not yet an exact

4   The Brouwersgracht, Amsterdam

science, while, indeed, it was not far removed from alchemy, and remembering those old patrician houses that reflect their swags and pilasters in the still or leaf-strewn water, down both embankments of the Rapenburg, we welcome two items of information given us by an English writer upon Holland: that Emanuel Gulliver was a graduate of Leyden, and that lodgings for students are advertised in windows, even to this day, as *cubicula locanda*. But Leyden is not much, it is a little only, of old Holland. The ghosts, less of Oxford or Cambridge than of Cracow or Bologna, are pertaining to it, of Cracow, particularly, where in his youth Dr Faustus was a student. And so from Leyden, by thought of its native Rembrandt and his portraits to the old towns of Holland, and to the canals where so much of mystery hides behind the plain façades.

It must be accepted that Holland in matters of architecture is of a chilly welcome. Her charities are private and not public, and may consist of no more than the light of a passage reflected through an overdoor. Nothing is given away in superabundant vitality of sunlight, as in Italy or Spain, where there may be much to dispense, but it is mostly outward show. Such are the grander houses in Dutch towns, but whatever their proportions there is perpetual fantasy in the fanlights. The tendency was for the fanlight to grow higher in order to allow more design, and an Englishman remembering the 'Adam' fanlights of London, or of Georgian Dublin, will not be long in forming a collection of the Dutch fanlights in his mind. They are of carved wood, painted white or cream, sometimes with gilding, and exhibit none of the English ambition to be correct and classical. The earlier examples are of simple Baroque scrolls and curves, till we get to elaborate monograms reminding us of the joined cyphers of William and Mary upon the keystones of the garden front of Hampton Court. It would appear that these must be superimposed upon the glass and that the pane is not cut to fit them. The fanlights are found all over Holland. So rich are the designs that they are enough, in themselves, to ornament a whole building, and nothing more is needed except the carving on the roof line. We may find that they look

5 *An interior in Amsterdam*

most fanciful, as was intended, upon a winter evening. Then the light streams out upon the leafless trees and upon the cobbled sidewalk. It may even reach to the dark waters of the canal. It heightens the mystery of the houses and makes us long, more than ever, to know what painted rooms or stucco work, for we have heard the rumours, may hide within.

By 'Dutch Renaissance' is intended the 'strapwork' style of such architects as Vredeman de Vries or Lieven de Key, who built the Meat Market at Haarlem, a manner of architecture with flat scrolled ornaments and obelisks galore. But in most Dutch towns this has been superseded by the multitude of later houses. Or we could say that there are not so many of the stepped gables, but, instead, in simple language, the houses have tops like Charles II mirror frames. Their character can be summarized as a stepped entrance with single or double ramp of stairs and tradesmen's entrance below; a ground floor; a flight of two floors above made into a single member, architecturally, by the flat pilasters that frame them; swags of fruit or flowers below the upper windows; and then the top storey with that aperture for a crane to hoist up coal and firewood which is the one enduring feature of all Dutch houses, old and new, this being framed in that blank mirror, or it could be compared, also, to a high chair back. There are rows and rows of houses of this type. For this is, indeed, the Dutch house on a canal.

But the Dutch Rococo is beginning. It manifests itself in delightful spray-like crestings to the gables. They become Rococo chair backs or mirror frames. It is not long before there are dolphins leaping in the spray. Those trim edgings to the gables that were characteristic of the earlier period and resembled the outer row of curls of a periwig, the spread curls of the periwig of a person sitting in the chair or looking into the mirror, have disappeared to make way for ornaments of sea shells and coats-of-arms. Soon, Neptune and his trident, mermen and maidens, or a naked Venus stand up against the northern sky. Mars, or the more warlike heroes, do not occur often, if at all. It was the sea imagery that appealed to Dutchmen, and is this any wonder? Negroes and

feathered Indians make an appearance too. But the Dutch allow
their fantasy to run riot in the front door and the fanlight. The
iron railings, as well, are most elaborate in some instances. But the
front doors offer the richest carving and coffering in wood, and can
be complete expressions of the solider, heavier trend of Rococo.
The entire unit or centre of the house becomes one body of
ornament, doorway, and bigger and lesser windows above that, all
forming one Rococo composition framed in flowing curves and
lines, and leading the eye to the crested gable that rises in the
centre of the roof line.

The destruction of old houses, all over Holland, has been as
bad as in England; notably the many superb houses that were
such prized possessions of Rotterdam, a city that was on the crest
of the wave in the eighteenth century, and were nearly utterly
demolished during the bombardment of Rotterdam in May 1940
when nearly all the old merchants' houses by the canals were
destroyed. An English architect who went, 30, but it is now more
than 50 years ago, to make drawings for an intended work on
Amsterdam, has told me that nearly all his chosen subjects have
now disappeared. And it is no new holocaust. A Frenchman, Henri
Havard, writing of the old city of Dordrecht in 1878, says: 'Here,
as elsewhere, the number of old buildings diminishes apace.
General indifference . . . the needs of commerce, the demands of
"comfort" lead each year to the disappearance of some one or
other of the old buildings. But, ere they vanish, Mijnheer van G.,
a learned son of Dordrecht, makes drawings of them. He has
indulged me with a sight of his huge portfolios, in which he has
carefully embalmed a hundred venerable, elegant, artistic or
curious façades, which have been destroyed within half a century'.
At that date, certainly, buildings of the eighteenth century will
have been allowed no quarter, and Dordrecht is an example of
what has happened throughout Holland. Unfortunately, too, the
big old eighteenth-century houses are of just the size and plan to
make good modern offices. Painted rooms interfere with desks and
counters, while a lift well takes up less room than an old staircase.
The entrance corridor and its plasterwork may be spared and,

perhaps, one room for the directors' meetings. Succeeding generations destroyed these rooms, too, with the changing fashions. But we will come to the painted rooms, in detail, in our account of Amsterdam.

The Dutch town, in general, was solid but unreal. It must be recalled, too, that their riches came to them from so far away, and that they had become wealthy in one generation. At the same time, the character of the water town did not alter. It was antique already, and we have now to prove, by example, that it was no new thing in Europe. Venice is, of course, the supreme instance of the water town, dating, in its origins, from the eighth and ninth centuries. But nothing is to be gained by seeking to compare Amsterdam and Venice in our minds, and we forbear from doing so. For there is only one Venice. During the Middle Ages Milan was nearly a water town, and even a map of the present day shows a canal surrounding most of the perimeter of the old city. Chartres is another, probably unsuspected, example of the old water town. It has three concentric canals or branches of the River Eure, which once nearly, if not quite, girdled the whole town. Amiens, upon the River Somme, has a network of eight or ten lines of canals in the lower end of the town, and its plan would not look out of place in Holland. But Strasbourg can be seen on any plan as lying entirely on an island, two miles from the Rhine, surrounded by two large arms of the Ill, and receiving the waters of the great canals that join respectively the Rhone and Rhine, and Marne and Rhine. Anciently, the town was crisscrossed and intersected by numerous small channels and canals, the unblocked ends of which lie stagnant below the old timber houses, matching the magpie buildings with their Pied Piper waters. Strasbourg, one of the most beautiful old towns in Europe – dare we say this? – belongs, aesthetically, to neither Celt nor Teuton, having been during the three most crucial centuries of its existence independent under the rule of its prince bishops. Strasbourg, and Alsace generally, must be conceded a neutral culture of their own.

Returning to The Netherlands, we shall find that there are ports and river towns, as well as water towns. Liège, for an instance, is a river town upon the Meuse and Ourthe. Antwerp is a seaport upon the Scheldt. It compares with Rotterdam upon the Meuse or Maas. Liège, that is to say, is another Namur or Mons. It is a town upon a river bank. But Antwerp and Rotterdam are sea-going ports upon a river, like London upon the Thames. But Bruges, Ghent, Malines to less degree, are complete water towns. They are the Flemish water towns.

A plan of Bruges or Ghent reveals the true complexity of their waters. Ghent lies on the Rivers Scheldt and Lys, but there are at least five or six arms or branches of those rivers. Bruges is described as lying upon the River Reie, but it seems to be a town, purely, of canals and bridges. That, indeed, was the reason for its name, which in Flemish means, quite simply, 'bridges'. These are the two towns in which to study the difference between the Flemish and the Dutch. They are medieval towns. Their greatness had passed from them before that of the Dutch began. Of the era of Rubens there is little evidence in these two cities. There are some later buildings at Bruges with gilt enrichments in the style of the fantastic guild houses in the Grand' Place at Brussels, and other dwellings of the early eighteenth century that have an air of peculiar melancholy, and long sash windows, a melancholy that bespeaks the swan-haunted waters of the Minnewater or lac d'Amour, and the elms and whitewashed houses of the Béguinage. When the leaves fall on the canals Bruges has a sadness all its own, a depression, though, that is not only true of Flanders. If you have seen an old Dutch town, like Delft, in October or November you have the feeling of utter stagnation and decay. It is typical of this little city that it should be at its most beautiful in the late evening, and I can think of it no differently now that I have seen it on a summer morning in the droning heat, but then the carillon began playing from the high steeple of the Nieuwekerk, the bells echoing all over the town from every shop window and from the walls of every house, and such a curious choice of tunes, 'Down, down on the Range', when last I was in Delft. In Amsterdam, too, you have only to listen for a moment and you will hear a barrel organ, of the kind peculiar to the Netherlands, an affair of pipes and drums, wound with the full force of one arm, pushed by three men, and with a great frontispiece of white wood, carved and painted, an organ that plays waltzes, Dutch clog dances, and mock-Spanish tangos, and that, once heard, gives a new meaning to the canals of Amsterdam.

But we would look at the plan of Delft. Its canals are like the bars of a gridiron, and the gridiron's handle. It resembles that implement far more nearly than does the Escorial, laid out, according to popular belief, in Spain, to represent the gridiron on which St Lawrence suffered martyrdom, and with the royal apartments of Philip II standing for the handle. Delft, besides the canal that frames it on all four sides, has five or six cross canals, in both directions. Amsterdam has its three principal canals, the Prinsengracht, the Keizergracht, and Heerengracht, that are entirely concentric and that turn an angle together six times. The Hague is more sparse of waters. The Vijver is another Minnewater, or lac d'Amour. But we will examine the plans of other towns. Haarlem has its River Spaarne flowing through it in a double curve, and a few canals. Utretcht is on the Rhine, which divides here, into the Old Rhine and the Vecht. Besides that, two canals flow through it, the Oude and the Nieuwe Gracht, canals which have the peculiarity that the houses are built so high above them that the ground floors below the wharves are used as living-rooms. Even Leeuwarden and Groningen, lying in that northern part of Holland which is not characteristic of the kingdom, or which has a separate and distinct character of is own, are surrounded by waters and are true water towns with canals, both big and small. Dordrecht is as waterbound as any town in Holland. The Old Meuse or Oude Maas flows round it, and the view of its canals, without quays or wharves but giving directly on the waters, may more nearly resemble the *piccoli canali* of Venice than those of any other town in Holland. Middelburg, in the island of Walcheren, has probably the most perfect of all water plans. It has a circular road enclosing the heart of the old town, and two lines of canals that are concentric, but the outer one has curves and salients as though for purposes of defence, so that its plan has been compared by one authority to that of Vauban's water citadel at Lille and been attributed to the hand of Coehoorn (1641–1704), Director-General of the fortresses of the States of Holland. Middelburg, Delft, Dordrecht, are typical Dutch towns. They are as Dutch as Amsterdam, which only exhibits the same particularities upon a bigger scale. But small towns and villages, in hundreds, have all the national character of Holland. They are canal towns, familiar with *tjalken, boeiers, pramen, schuiten, aken, botteks, schouwen* – all the flotilla of Dutch water craft.

Some few of the bigger towns, Utrecht, Dordrecht, Leyden, Delft and Haarlem, the two capitals apart, may be all that the foreigner will see of Holland. These towns, and the Dutch picture galleries, are a part of common knowledge, and it is not easy to find new things to say of them. The more subtle secrets which are our subject and even, in part, of our own finding will come later. There is little, for instance, in Utrecht except its fine museum. But, next door to that, in the adjoining building, we may gain our first experience of the eighteenth century in Holland. It is one of the *hofjes,* almshouses or orphanages, a feature in Dutch towns, and often among the most delightful buildings in any of their cities. The particular *hofje* of which we are writing is an orphanage founded by a Baroness van Reede van Renswoude, and exhibiting some traces of an Austrian or German Baroque influence, not only in the stone façade, but in the large hall on the first floor that resembles the Kaisersaal in some monastery in Bavaria or down the Danube, a room in cream and green and gold, with a portrait of the foundress, much heraldry and gilt enrichment, and even the porcelain service bearing her coat-of-arms upon which banquets are served, upon occasion, to the guardians or trustees. The cleanliness of the staircase and corridor with their waxed floors is not to be described in words; but the body of local noblemen who were trustees of this Utopian establishment, one of the aims of which was to train orphans to become painters, is assembled in another room in two large paintings, and one can only say of these pictures that one has never seen so many wigs together, or so many jocund, smiling faces. These convivial, kindly gentlemen of Utrecht we will meet later in their villas on the Vecht, in days when that river was a stage upon the Grand Tour and a highway into Europe.

Were we asked what other building in Utrecht to consider, for the cathedral is not much, it is but half a Gothic church, we would choose a certain house, Jans-Kerkhof 13, for this is an absolute model of a Dutch house of the golden period. It much resembles, indeed, the Mauritshuis and suggests The Hague, just as the tree-lined square of the Jans-Kerkhof will recall the Lange Voorhout when we search along that for old houses. The Mauritshuis is by Jacob van Campen, and close comparison of the two houses so much fortifies the resemblance that we wonder if Pieter Post was not architect of Jans-Kerkhof 13. Both have the same pediment, the same swags of fruit, and the same number of windows in the elevation. The differences are that the Mauritshuis has stone pilasters throughout, and is the more expensive building. Unfortunately the interior of this house at Utrecht, now a bank, has been entirely modernized, but when we think how much more of this historic city has gone utterly we can but be sadder still.

The destruction at Dordrecht, already alluded to when we mentioned its hecatomb of old buildings, has but spared a house or two. One that remains is an example of how noble a plain brick house may be made by the use of pilasters and simple swags of fruit. It has not even been necessary to difference the windows, and the doorway is not exceptional. The pilasters are ornament enough for the whole building. How Dutch it is! Another lovely and dignified old building is that of the Dordrechtsche Courant, an old printing office, Grootekerkplein 3, where we admire the sober, flat brick pilasters, the crested window cases and swags of fruit below, and dolphin'd overdoor. Both these Dordrecht houses may be the work of Pieter Post the younger. The master printer lives two doors away, in an old house with good stucco-work and Louis XVI panelling in one room, where mirrors, overdoors, and ceiling decoration are of carved wood, not plaster. But the old town of Dordrecht can be but the phantom of what it used to be. We could almost say that all it has left, now, is the beauty of its situation on a point of land surrounded on all sides by the water. The quiet golden tones of Cuyp are a memory of his native Dordrecht and its polders. The Grootekerk, the old houses, what few of them are left, and the canals ever compose themselves into his long golden afternoons and evenings, until old Dordrecht, we come to understand, was a world to itself and all sufficient for one lifetime.

If it be possible, for it is our intention at present to look at Haarlem without Frans Hals, we would begin with the ship models of the seventeenth century that hang up in St Bavo's, and listen to the organ. There can be few buildings in the world in which a Bach prelude and fugue sound more imposing than in this grandest of all Dutch churches. We would listen, were there opportunity, to fugues by Buxtehude and by the Dutchman Sweelinck, who lies buried in the Oudekerk at Amsterdam, and remember, too, that Mozart played upon this organ. But the rest of Haarlem, for our purposes, consists of the Meat Market, and the Almshouses. The Meat Market is contemporary to our Wollaton or Hardwick Hall, to Longleat or Montacute. It is the master-piece of Lieven de Key, and whether we like it or not, one of the great and typical buildings of the Northern Renaissance. The material is brick and stone, and nowhere else are there such elaborate stepped gables. You could run up the steps easily, were it not for so many pointed, pricking obelisks. The side range of the Meat Market, next to St Bavo's, is more elaborate, even, than the part of the building facing upon the square. It has three fretted and tremendous gables, with obelisks in all variety; those that rise from a base shaped like an armillary sphere, the squat sort that are broad and blunt, and the long thin ones ending in a ball which is pierced by the fine point of the obelisk. The Meat Market must have looked very fanciful in the architect's drawing, and it may be that we should regard it less as a building than as Dutch cabinet work of the most capricious kind. The Frans Hals Museum (we look at the museum for the moment without the paintings) is by Lieven de Key also.* It is an almshouse, the Oudemannenhuis, a name that, for once in Holland, it is not difficult to understand.

* This attribution to Lieven de Key is disputed by some authorities.

There is a fine Rococo overmantel in one of the rooms, with cupids and a picture frame above. The Regentenkamer in the Hofje van Noblet, an easy name also, has a fireplace with grisaille painting over it; and we come to the Hofje van Staats te Haarlem, a beautiful brick building, with wooden belfry, like an old Town Hall in England, and in one room a delightful painting of the Regents, two notaries in white lappets looking at the plan, a quill pen held by another, and a fourth grand person, all in great periwigs, a group of robust and kindly Dutchmen who must be companions, in another world, of Captain Coram.

Leyden is the most beautiful of the old water towns. Its atmosphere, which we have attempted to distil upon one of our first pages, may be implicit from the moment when we hear the name, or pass the inn sign, of In den Vergulden Turk (The Golden Turk). The Stadhuis by Lieven de Key, next door, is like an urban version of Bolsover Castle with its obelisks and pinnacles, and the near prospect, not of collieries, but trams. But the sensation of Leyden quickens into ineffable loveliness in the rose-petal brick interior of the Pieterskerk.

Leyden, as would be expected, has many fine old buildings. For an example, the Hofje van Broekhoven, Papengracht 16, with a little stone frontispiece, rare in Holland, of four Doric pilasters rising from a base, coupled together by swags of fruit, blank panels to either side of the doorway with vertical swags and an empty niche below, well-weighted cornice, pediment, and high pitched roof, a perfect instance of good manners from the seventeenth century, the age of courtesy, to the infirm or old or orphaned, and an aesthetic pleasure to all passers-by. But, in Leyden, our steps are drawn insistently along both quays of the Rapenburg; to the pair of mirror-back houses in the style of Vingboons; to the three seventeenth-century houses grouped together under one roof line; to numbers 8 to 10, one house only, in reality, of finest conceivable laid brick, each single brick, as only in the light of Holland, standing out separately, as though in a painting by Jan van der Heyden, with a truly magnificent swag of fruit and flowers surrounding the central window; or to 48, our own favourite, with its half a dozen flat Doric pilasters, joined by swags, great wide windows upon either floor, and hardly any wall, so sensible a prevision in an inclement climate. The good taste of the period speaks out in the proportion and in its sober, modest bearing among so many other houses of that golden age of building.

The prevailing date of the houses along the Rapenburg at Leyden is about 1670 or 1680. One beautiful little building, now a museum of engravings,* is earlier and there are the buildings of the university, and some later houses. The Rapenburg, itself, is wider than most Dutch canals; but not one of these towns except Dordrecht can be described in terms of view or landscape. There are no fine perspectives, no view of the dome of St Paul's across the curving river, none of the spires of our city churches, and it would be entirely ridiculous to attempt a comparison with Venice, for there is no more similarity than that all the cities named are built upon canals. There are the picture galleries which we should keep for rainy days. But it is more profitable to admire the stalls of the flower vendors, irises, roses, gladioli, in their season. We soon learn in Dutch towns to look for unsensational, quiet buildings, and to enquire for the almshouses or *hofjes*. It is then that we realize, perhaps upon passing for the second time, how much taste and experience have been demanded for their simple buildings. It is with the same sensation that a cabinet picture by Maes or by Metsu may recall you in front of it, and then, suddenly, we may come upon the house of a patrician, of a Pieter de Hooch, and we are left to wonder at the mystery of these old Dutch dwellings and their inhabitants. These old towns are not, we reiterate, the most interesting things in Holland. They have been seen, again and again, by successive generations of travellers of all nations. There is little or nothing to be gained by attempting a routine description, since this is not a guide book. But Dordrecht by any standard of comparison is beautiful, and we would have Leyden and its old houses upon the Rapenburg as romantic as we can make them.

* The Bibliotheca Thysiana is by the town architect, Arent van 's-Gravesande.

3. Amsterdam

If we would enquire into the difference between Amsterdam and London, it is that Amsterdam has no fogs, only sea mists, and that in the working-class suburbs there are flowers in every window. It is, in the first place, the immensity of London that appals the foreigner. Amsterdam is a much lesser town than London. Its fine old houses are confined to a small area, almost, we might say, to the area of the three famous canals, the Heeren, Keizers and Prinzengracht, 'the houses along the Keizersgracht being less impressive than those of the Heerengracht though towards the end of the eighteenth century the former was nevertheless considered the better address', *Apollo*, November 1972. But the interior mystery of London has often intrigued the foreigner. And there was the London fog, an obscurity such as the present generation has not known, the dark of 'black out' being of a different opacity from fog. We will take an opinion, that of a great musician. This is what Ferruccio Busoni has to say of the capital of England : 'London is always beautiful, whether in sunshine or in fog. I should describe London architecture as cautious . . . even in their buildings the English want not to attract notice . . . the architecture stands out as a quiet and firm background to history, that I call strength and victory.' These words were written in 1919;* and they are true of 1946. One of the few and fast diminishing old London interiors, a solicitor's office, shall we say, somewhere near Lincoln's Inn Fields or Bedford Square, the part

---

* Cf. *Ferruccio Busoni*, by Edward J. Dent, London, Oxford University Press, 1933, p. 242.

of London most akin to Amsterdam, would show this typical reticence and understatement in the 'Adam' mantelpiece, or the classical motifs of urn and honeysuckle in low relief upon the stucco ceiling. There is nothing, here, of the Dutch delight in living. For this, we shall find in Holland, is what lies hidden, unsuspected.

But Amsterdam has old houses to be seen in hundreds, among the earliest of them being the twin buildings of the Gouden and Zilveren Spiegel or the Gold and Silver Mirrors, in the Kattegat, a pair of inns or public houses dating from 1614, which is an early date for Amsterdam, typical red brick houses with wooden shutters and stepped gables. Here, the comparison is not with London or Venice. It is between Dutch and German. This little pair of buildings is Teutonic in feeling, even though tempered by the Dutch humanity, and it may be added in terms of commodity, 'small beer', only just worth the walk and the adventure of enquiring for them.

Philippe and Justus Vingboons, great names in Holland, were architects of some of the old mirror-back houses. But Justus Vingboons, upon occasion, could be more mundane or of the world at large. His house for Mijnheer Trip, Kloveniersburgwal 29, is a palace with a flight of flat Corinthian pilasters, eight in number, above a plain ground floor, elaborate swags and garlands below the windows, a rich cornice and a pediment. A private 'palace' as understood in Italy or Austria, in Germany or in France; but we may think that it is Dutch, none the less, and could only stand on a canal.* Philippe Vingboons, for his influence in forming the Dutch houses, is the most important of the architects at Amsterdam. Jacob van Campen is too correct, too little Dutch, by contrast. The Royal Palace, formerly, and more appropriately, the Town Hall, displays his heavy, unimaginative hand, not lightened by the sculptures of Artus Quellin and his family on the exterior pediments or in the many rooms and halls within.

* Justus Vingboons, in association with Simon de la Vallée, was architect of the delightful *Riddarhus*, or House of Lords, in Stockholm. It was built to the order of Queen Christina of Sweden, and is the finest building in the Swedish capital.

Adriaan Dorstman is a more agreeable designer, who favoured a flat façade of French character, with level cornice and no gables, but keeping the Dutch stepped entrance. A few of his houses stand on the Keizersgracht and Heerengracht to be known, at once, by their French feeling.

But we turn a corner of the Prinsengracht and there, in front of us, is the most Dutch-looking of all churches that could be imagined. It is the Westerkerk, begun by Hendrik de Keyser in 1620, with a tower that is the earlier prototype of London city churches, but what is peculiarly Dutch in this high red brick building is its enormous gables. This is the last work of de Keyser, who did not live to see it finished, and it is a building which we should say in England belonged to the middle of the century or later. Not altogether unexpectedly it reminds us of the riding school at Bolsover; it is what we would call Dutch Louis xiii or Charles i, in the sense in which the building, just mentioned, foreshadows and anticipates developments that come to nothing and had no architectural progeny, transitional work done during the pause or interval between two styles. However, in the instance of the Westerkerk it is one of the most perfect examples of the Dutch genius in building, a magical synthesis of the Elizabethan and the Carolean, yet with time and individuality of its own. For the Westerkerk is as eloquent of Holland as some bare whitewashed mosque that could be Mohammedan and nothing else, the Dutch Reformed Church having, at that time, the white-hot fervency of the pure Moslems. Its gables, we have said, are immensely high, framed with pilasters of stone upon their upper storeys, topped with stone urns, above which rise the high dormers to the roof line, a pair of great gables with a lesser one, between, to both flanks of the church, and a similar high gable for the west end. Within, the Westerkerk is bare and uncompromising as all Dutch churches, but with the usual extraordinary array of 'banks' or grandstands intended, in the true meaning of that word, for the 'bigwigs' of the congregation. Nothing else in the Westerkerk, except a pair of painted organ shutters with beautiful trophies of drums and lutes, and the knowledge that Rembrandt's bones lie buried here. Church interiors by Pieter

Saenredam or Emanuel de Witte, the former a considerable painter in a genre in which it might be deemed impossible to be original, or anything but a delineator of costume and architecture, depict the long services in the Dutch churches, but really the congregations must have demanded a satirist or caricaturist to themselves. All the population went to church; and coming out of the Westerkerk we can only reflect that odd as may have been the scenes in church upon a Sunday morning, it must have been more curious still when not a living soul except the old or ill, or Jews, were in their houses, and from all over the town, in snow or sleet, in rain or sunshine, there rose the sound of psalm singing on the eternal Sabbath air.

The Oudekerk, or part of it when I last saw it in 1947, was one great charnel house of bones. A horrible, black, porous soil was heaped up in one aisle, out of which protruded skulls and thigh bones, fragments of arms and legs, and bony digits, all thrown together but without shreds of flesh or any covering. Most of these, no doubt, had been rich or noble persons in their day. Both here and in the Nieuwekerk there are huge marble monuments to admirals. De Ruyter, who died of wounds received at Syracuse, has a tomb in this latter church by Rombout Verhulst with the usual admiral's crown or naval coronet formed from a five-fold cluster of ship's boats. Tromp lies in a similar tomb in the Ouderkerk at Delft, and most of these memorials to admirals have marble reliefs of naval battles, which are the best parts of the monuments. In other respects the tombs, generally, are monotonous, and with a few exceptions, which we hope to illustrate, much inferior to English sculptures of the same date. The Dutch churches, into which it is always troublesome to enter, are disappointing too, except for the few instances that we shall mention.

The Westerkerk, at least, is a fine church, but not romantic, and massy of bullion, of ducats and doubloons, like the synagogue of the Portuguese Jews. This is at once one of the simplest and most impressive brick edifices in all Holland, standing in a forecourt of low, dark, brick buildings and in the shade of ancient trees. A plain brick exterior; but, within, it is one great hall with a double row of stone columns, pillars that are as splendid as great trees, huge wooden women's galleries that run round the building, and a glittering, shining array of brass chandeliers, wall lights, and mere brass candlesticks fastened to the wooden benches. Probably in no other building in the world is there such a collection of objects of polished brass. The splendid *hechal* or cupboard to hold the rolls of the law in their embroidered coverings is designed like some great architectural frontispiece, with pillars supporting obelisks and bold cornices and architraves, the material being jacaranda wood brought from Brazil. It is an interior, were that possible, in the Rembrandt manner, completed by the architect Adriaan Dorstman* and dedicated in 1676 after Rembrandt was dead, but his friends had been Jews, he painted often from Jewish models, lived by preference in the Jewish quarter, and we may imagine for ourselves how much the scene in the synagogue would have appealed to Rembrandt.

For these are the Sephardim, *Sepharda* signifying Spain and Portugal in Hebrew, and we have to think of the elderly Rabbis, with long beards, in purple or violet caftans and still wearing the Andalucian wide-brimmed sombrero. The more devout of the Jews would have the *taled,* a white square veil with strings and tassels, called the *zizith,* upon their heads, and the *tessilin* or phylacteries upon their foreheads enclosing cabbalistic texts or sentences sewn up in them. Some will have covered themselves all over with these strings and tassels. In the *Cérémonies Réligieuses* of Picart, a work of 1710 in which there are several plates depicting the ceremonies of the Portuguese Jews of Amsterdam, we read that 'Jews of a piety above the common standard have sometimes carried the devotion of the *tessilin* into the bridal bed; a wise and ingenious contrivance to sanctify an action, where sanctity seems very hardly practicable; and where, too, the most solid piety runs the risk of falling into strange distractions.'†

* It was begun by Elias Bouman.

† Mr Cecil Roth, the well-known authority on Jewish history, informs me of the eighteenth-century dress with knee-breeches and three-cornered hats, worn with beards by the members of this synagogue until the recent war.

6   *The Hofje, Breda*

7   *Zundert*

The Jews had for centuries been encouraged to live in Portugal and rose to positions of great eminence in the Middle Ages. Proof of this is to be seen in the pair of great tryptychs by Nuno Gonçalves in the gallery at Lisbon, painted in about 1460, portraying Alfonso v of Portugal, Prince Henry the Navigator, and the leading personalities of the day, for beside the Priors of Alcobaça and Batalha stands the figure of a Rabbi, to be known by his hat and beard and Jewish countenance. It is a curious sensation to recognize a member of this most ancient of races in this tryptych by the Portuguese primitive, for persons of this identical type are to be seen in paintings by Carpaccio and Gentile Bellini at Venice. Their dress and racial type are distinct from that of the Oriental merchants in silken gowns and turbans; they, in fact, resemble the figure of Agrippa in *Struwwelpeter,* and seem to fulfil some childhood memory in their dress and feature. They were expelled from Portugal in 1496, only four years after the Jews were turned out of Spain, settling first in Antwerp, to be driven thence by the Spaniards, and migrating to Amsterdam in 1576, bringing with them their industry of diamond-polishing. Arriving in Holland they continued to speak Portuguese until less than 100 years ago, and are still called by Portuguese names, but they were, of course, hideously persecuted during World War II, and but few of their number are still surviving. Hitler at the height of his infamous powers contrived and allowed the deaths of some 100,000 of these industrious citizens of Holland. This is but one of the outrages that will for ever blacken his evil name.

No exaggeration is intended when we describe the synagogue of the Portuguese Jews as having the most noble interior in Amsterdam. For it is a magnificence that is intrinsic in its proportions and rich ornament. The synagogue of the Spanish and Portuguese Jews at Bevis Marks, in Aldgate, is said to be a copy and this, also, is a fine building, but it falls short of the original. There is not, in fact, much resemblance between them except that both are temples of the Jewish faith, and not churches. Among the congregation in Amsterdam would be men of learning, Samuel Menasseh ben Israel, or his like, who came to London on a mission to Cromwell, or Ephraim Bonus the physician and alchemist, both of them subjects of etched portraits from the hand of Rembrandt. The Portuguese Jews were in close communication with the Spanish Jews of Smyrna and Salonica, and these walls will have heard the rumours of Sabbathai Zevi, the false Messiah, himself a Spanish Jew, on whose behalf in 1666, the Messianic year, books were printed in Amsterdam describing the ceremonial for his crowning, laying down the prayers to use, and the proper manner in which to address him. Some of the Jews of Hamburg, in the words of a contemporary, 'were having their hair cut so as to be able to hear the blast of the Messiah's horn more easily'. After the persecutions of the war it is something of a miracle that the synagogue is still standing, and has not been entirely deserted and demolished. It is the noblest building in Amsterdam, and among the splendid interiors of the seventeenth century that have come down to us. In all Europe, this synagogue of the Portuguese Jews has a place apart; this, without consideration of the history of this most interesting and enduring of minorities.*

Already it has become an enchantment to stroll along the Keizersgracht and Heerengracht, canals which are entirely concentric and which turn an angle together six times, and to conjecture which will be the houses we would choose to enter. The old houses of Amsterdam so closely resemble the older parts of London. It could till not long ago be paralleled by passing a morning in the squares and terraces of Bloomsbury, or a whole day in Bath. We may know that they have fine interiors but it is little comfort if we cannot go inside. The houses are so much alike that it is confusing. So many have been spoilt or modernized, and they are too numerous to go round from door to door. Less even than in London is there in Amsterdam any clue as to which are the street numbers of the fine old houses, for the Dutch have hardly begun to admire their eighteenth century. As a consequence of this, during previous visits the present writer did not

* The old cemetery of the Portuguese Jews at Oude Kerk, five miles from Amsterdam, upon the Amstel, has a number of fine tomb-slabs and must be worth a visit.

see a single interior upon either the Keizersgracht or Heerengracht. They are not mentioned in any guide book; Dutch is a difficult tongue for the foreigner to read, even if the Dutch possess this printed information; and in general the Dutch themselves are not interested and point only to the house of Rembrandt in the Joden-Breestraat.

But we are sufficiently primed to choose for ourselves and make a beginning. We have noticed, even during the conventional tour of the canals in a crowded motor boat, a certain house with posts and chains outside it, an elaborate flight of steps, and from canal level, an entrance hall in white stucco with a bust in a periwig above an inner door. We identify it as a house upon the Heerengracht, take a note of its street number, and find it to be the headquarters of the British Information Services. Coming in, up the entrance steps, the hall has those magnificent carvings in stucco that we observed from the water, the bust is on its pedestal above the door, and we are seeing for the first time a splendid Dutch interior of the eighteenth century. Many of the Dutch houses have not this entrance hall. They lead straight on to a passage, and in fact, this typical Dutch corridor with stucco enrichments upon the walls follows as soon as you have walked through the inner door, and below that sculptured periwig. This seems to be the unvarying plan for Dutch houses of the later period, and it is found throughout the country from Friesland to Limburg. So ubiquitous, too, are the Dutch habits of kindness and hospitality, particularly towards Englishmen, that at sight of a house of this character in any town it becomes a habit to push open the front door – they are always kept ajar – and admire the stucco work along the corridor.

A good staircase is not so invariable a feature. We shall find that the stairs in these later houses can be of the utmost magnificence, upon one or two occasions at Amsterdam, but, above all, in the grand stairways by Daniel Marot at The Hague, stairwells ascending the whole height of the house and culminating in a cupola or lantern. In the house we are visiting upon the Heerengracht – and how the Dutch love to roll that 'r' and put in a guttural 'h' for the 'g', till the 'gracht' becomes a password between the Dutch themselves, but a shibboleth to foreigners! – the stairway is unexceptional. The larger town houses in Amsterdam, approximating to great old houses in Berkeley Square or Grosvenor Square, may have as many as four big rooms upon the ground floor, two at the front and two at the back, besides the entrance hall, the corridor and stairwell. Upstairs there will be four more rooms of the same size. There will be a garden at the back, and probably a garden pavilion or summerhouse. Whole rows of these latter must have stood, at one time, behind the houses on both banks of the Keizersgracht and Heerengracht.

The first painted rooms at Amsterdam may have been by Adam Pynacker (1622-73). Panels from the hand of this forgotten artist decorated the walls of many of the old burgher houses. By the time of Descamps, towards the middle of the next century, hardly any were remaining, and in 1820 only one house still had a painted room by Pynacker. In the next generation Gerard de Lairesse (*d.* 1711), who had the greatest of reputations in his day, painted ceilings and wall panels for many houses. These, too, in their turn were nearly all destroyed. There followed the more decorative painters of the eighteenth century, minor artists, it may be, but in Holland, where so high a level of technical competence prevailed, these are often perfect exemplars of what a painted room can be. For it is a genre to itself, like that of garden sculpture, demanding poetry and imagination but not the highest gifts of all. The painted rooms, not works in fresco, but either upon panel or upon prepared canvas fastened directly upon the walls, are one of the aesthetic delights of Holland. But so insistent is the fame of Dutch cabinet pictures, often of low merit and no better than the works of mid-Victorian painters of the fifties and sixties, that the existence of this Dutch school of decorative painting is not recorded. We have to assume that the surviving number of these rooms may be but the tenth part of the total, for they have been destroyed, indiscriminately, without a hand lifted to defend them. It is to be remarked, further, that being the works of Dutchmen they are pursued, carefully, to the utmost detail. Probably every patrician or rich burgher house had at least one painted room, and with equal probability this would be the first room to fall victim to the holocaust. The present house on the Heerengracht is no exception. Only one room has been preserved intact, the back room on the left ground floor, foretaste of many other interiors in Amsterdam, The Hague, and all over Holland, a saloon with a great mantelpiece in green and gold, heraldic shields, gold scrollwork, and a fine stucco ceiling, not a painted room, but the panels were intended for cut velvet, or embossed and painted leather. This is all. Upon the first floor there is nothing. We come away in ignorance of the history of this old house, for as yet we do not know the name of the original owner, or the names of the architect or craftsmen.

Another beautiful old Amsterdam interior is Heerengracht 507, the old mansion of the Six van Hillegom family before they removed to their present house upon the Amstel. This was formerly the Six Museum, belonging to the descendants of Burgomaster Six, the friend of Rembrandt, and still containing the superb portrait by Rembrandt of the Burgomaster, perhaps the most wonderful of his portraits for its air of deep thought and contemplation, and it was not only on account of that mistaken address that this grand old interior came to our knowledge. The Six mansion has a façade that gives some hint of the rich stucco work inside, in the white stucco manner of Daniel Marcot and the old houses at The Hague. Baroque, therefore, and not Rococo in spirit, but it may be an indication of the neglect and apathy with which buildings of this date are still regarded in Holland that I have been able to find no description of the house in any written account of the Six Collection. That it contained paintings by Rembrandt of unique interest, as still belonging to the family, but was built 100 years later than his day, must be the reason for this silence. The mansion has now been turned into offices, but there are still the staircase, and the stuccos of the corridor. One or two of the rooms, also, have been left unspoilt; the stucco of the hall is of an extraordinary depth of cutting, yellowish in tone, and with its more than lifesize figures of pagon gods and goddesses is reminiscent of work of the Franchini brothers in Bath and Dublin, but richer and more

Baroque in air than was permitted by the English conscience. This old house is no less than a revelation of what lies hidden behind the solemn Dutch façades of Amsterdam.

But a yet more sumptuous interior is that of the 'Huize van Brienen', Heerengracht 284, belonging formerly to the family of that name. The modest exterior makes it more surprising still, for it has a front of three windows only, or even of a front door and two windows, while the entrance stair has but a single ramp. It is only the rich stone cresting to the roof, so rare in Amsterdam, with fine Rococo mantling and coat-of-arms, that draws attention, for in all other respects it is no more splendid than many other mansions upon the Heerengracht and Keizersgracht. The architect, it appears, was a Frenchman, Frédéric Blancard. The two rooms on the ground floor, front and back, are Louis XVI in date, with good furniture and mantelpieces, but let out, now, for offices. The entrance corridor has stucco work, without figures, and we go down the long passage to the stair. At foot of that, looking through a window to the right hand, there is a most beautiful little court; or rather, it is a blind wall decorated in the richest winter garden style in dove-grey and white, with a statue standing on a pedestal under a niche, while, above, the side piers that contain cupboards flow up into scrolled and curving ornaments of no purpose but mere fantasy and decoration. This little masterpiece of invention for a waste corner, so Dutch in spirit, but of the French manner of Louis XV, is worthy of the Place Stanislas at Nancy, where we might look for it behind a façade by Héré, or close to a black and gilt grille or balcony by Lamour. But we return to the stair, for this is exceptional; a carved wooden stair rail of richest possible design, rising, with lovely stair heads, for two floors, with a circular rotating motion, and, miraculously, no break at all, as though carved out in one flow of inspiration. This is, indeed, a superb example of woodcarving, of limewood, we would suggest, and eloquent of 1730, its date, in every detail. The carved wooden doors are no less splendid, consisting of a long panel, like a mirror case, and an overdoor with earlier Marot motifs, left over, if we may express that, from late Louis XIV, for that is their effect in dark wood, highly polished. Through one of these doors we enter a saloon with paintings by Dirk Dalens (1688-1753). It is not easy to describe this room. We will begin with the mantelpiece, which is not elaborate, but supports the richest of mirror frames in white-painted wood, the upper part or cornice of the glass being engraved with a motif like the Prince of Wales' feathers, and above, a simpler and smaller panel that frames a painting. This mantelpiece, from floor to ceiling, with its sham capitals to either side and triple or three-fold cornice, is a satisfying and beautiful composition. The ceiling is a painted panel, enclosed in what we would term a flowering octagon, for no pair of its sides is a straight line, while there are paintings in grisaille in the angles. The painted ceiling and the panel over the mantelpiece are by another hand, that of Anthonie Elliger* (1701-81): so are the little grisaille paintings. The painted panels on the walls are separated, in the angles of the room, by other panels like painted wings of scenery, these having for subject great urns or vases with a pair of cupids and fruit and flowers. The paintings upon the walls are of Italianate palaces in Dutch moats, and this tradition, deriving from a forgotten school of painting, through Adam Pynacker, Jan Both, Claes Berchem, Paul Brill, from all the Dutchmen who went to Italy, ends here, in this dining-room, in what is equivalent to a scenic wallpaper of the highest degree of excellence, and a decorative work, therefore, of the first order. The longer panel depicts an Italian coast scene with a high obelisk among the trees, indeterminate figures of peasants carrying baskets upon their heads to prove they are Italian, and Dutch cattle. But it is the smaller panels, to each side of the fireplace, that show the Claudian palaces set in moats; a pair of swans, in one, upon the near shore, close to a statue, and in the other, at foot of a tree, a great sunflower, roses and other flowers in which the spirit of the Dutchman comes through his Italian mannerisms, and on the bough of the tree, a hoopoe with black and white crest, cinnamon

* A painted ceiling with the Banquet of the Gods by A. Elliger is to be seen in one of the rooms at the Stedelijk Museum at Leyden. It was removed from a house at Arnhem and dates from 1730.

breast, and black and white barred wings and tail, looking out on a Palladian Isola Bella with ghostly portico and statues, but set in the weedy waters of a still Dutch moat. Of the painter, Dirk Dalens, we know nothing whatever, though this must be one of the prettiest of all painted rooms, and its Rococo elegance is a model for what can be accomplished by a minor talent. There were many such in Holland, as we hope to prove by word and illustration.

Heerengracht 475 is in another and more pompous manner. The hall has huge lifesize statues, and the stair, which is certainly influenced by Daniel Marot and his houses at The Hague, climbs to the top of the building, growing more ornate as it proceeds. Upon the staircase walls there are lifesize figures, in mezzo-relievo, emerging from panels that are like great mirror frames. We see the Muse of Comedy, mask in hand, and with a trumpet and plays, or rolls of music, at her feet. Upon the next wall is the figure of Orpheus playing his lute, and with a huge violoncello at his side. The fluted, banded pillars lend an unnecessary richness to the scene. But the top of the staircase well is no less than a concert in stucco. Upon its four walls, just below the vaulted ceiling, there is a simulated balcony with cloths thrown over it, round all four sides, and on each wall an entire band of musicians. They are playing flutes and mandolines, violins and cellos; in one, an Apollo, baton in hand, conducts the music; and in another a lifesize figure beats with his sticks upon a pair of kettledrums. We do not know the reason for this musical obsession, but it is so pronounced and taken to such lengths that it cannot be mere accident of choice. Music is definitely the subject of these stucco decorations. The musicians upon balconies are a translation into stucco from Italian frescoes. Tiepolo painted bands of musicians in so many of his frescoes, over doorways and on balconies, and it became a cliché, or set convention, with masters of architectural painting and perspective. Italian derivation is argued, therefore, but the stucco work is carried further than it would have been in Italy. The detail, at the same time, is French. But Heerengracht 475 has more to offer. A painted dining-room has been preserved with architectural subjects in a Dutch-Pannini manner, contrived so ingeniously that one of the canvases curves without break or tear and fits upon the door. The painter is Isaac de Moucheron (1670-1744), 'called "Ordonnance" on account of his cleverness in composition'. The few facts that can be given about this forgotten painter corroborate the date we have suggested for the stucco work. 'In 1694 he visited Rome, and made a number of drawings in the vicinity of Tivoli. . . . On his return to Amsterdam he was chiefly employed in painting large landscapes for the ornaments of saloons.' Judging from this example before us, 'Ordonnance' liked to paint rusticated pavilions or summerhouses by the side of ornamental water, and put in statues, clipped trees, flights of steps, and persons in pleasure boats, and once we know his mannerisms it is easy to distinguish him from his contemporary, Dirk Dalens.

These four interiors may be the most interesting of those still surviving in Amsterdam, but their very existence, as we have said, is only discovered with some difficulty. They may be known only to a handful of the Dutch themselves, comparing in this to the small public who have seen those London masterpieces of Kent and Adam, 44 Berkeley Square and 20 Portman Square. A comparison shows the greater exuberance of the Dutch examples. They are neither Palladian-Venetian, nor classical-Georgian. Three of the Amsterdam houses are in full-blooded Baroque, while the fourth, the 'Huize van Brienen', is of a grave and manly Rococo.

But the canals below the windows fed the imagination. From this dead level of the waters, in whatever direction the mind travelled, it led to fantasy. We believe this to be the reason for that 'inward exuberance and exterior restraint'. For such are characteristics that are still discernible in Amsterdam. We discover it upon hearing one of the barrel organs for the first time. But there are other signs, when we know how to look for them along the quiet canals. The Dutch, for instance, have a craze for Tzigane bands. (Alike, the barrel organs and the Gypsy bands are things of the past. During three days in Amsterdam in April 1973 not a barrel organ was to be seen or heard.) They are gone as completely as the painted carts that used to enliven the streets of Palermo. There was not one band of the sort in Brussels, but there were half a dozen in Amsterdam, Roumanian Gypsies, calling themselves Russians or Bessarabians, who by some miracle survived the war. No restaurant in Amsterdam was first rate without a Gypsy band. They played in a pretended Russian, Viennese, Hungarian manner, but betrayed their nationality when asked for 'Ciocarla' or for a *Hora*. The craving for this sort of music, and its association with enjoyment seems to be born in all Dutchmen. It is their escape from the prosaic, from the canal locks, and from a landscape that is so little evident that, so far, in 30 pages we have not mentioned it. Must it not be the same instinct that has made the Dutch into a race of florists? This is their compensation for lack of trees and mountains. But for those who love the old houses and canals of Amsterdam there are rewards at every moment, greatest perhaps when the canals are illuminated by myriads of white bulbs for some national festival. Then, if you take your stand at some strategic point you can see countless lights reflected in the water of several canals, with the lighted outlines of a number of bridges on each. It is a fairy scene that rejoices the heart as much as the eye, and makes one reflect how long deprivation of even lighted shop windows in wartime England played its part in depressing the spirit. Looking out from the window of a restaurant along the Leidschestraat, upon a summer evening, during dinner, you may see a couple of Volendammers coming over the bridge and, for a moment, you do not know who they can be, this man in baggy trousers and black jacket, and the young woman with him in her horned cap and blue and white skirt, walking like a Gypsy. Another evening, it is generally upon a Saturday or Sunday, it is a young woman of Urk. And in front of the railway station, of all drear buildings, sister to the Rijksmuseum, emanations, both of them, from the brain of Cuypers, the Sir Gilbert Scott of Amsterdam, there are always a group of Marken folk hurrying back to catch their boat or tram. In front of the old houses there are the flower stalls; there were barrel organs in the day; Gypsy bands at nightfall; and, by night and day, the endless beauties of her old buildings and her quiet canals.

During the 25 years that have elapsed since 1947, but more particularly of late, a good deal of research has been undertaken on the old houses of Amsterdam and The Hague. 'Documentary research has been carried on, designs have been brought to light and the subject of these old houses is increasingly in the public eye. Yet, we still lack, for instance, an inventory of surviving work of this kind in Amsterdam, the most important of Dutch cities.' J. W. Niemeijer in an article in *Apollo* for November 1972 dealing largely with the painted interiors of Amsterdam which were numerous in their day. The finest houses along the Heerengracht are Nos 168, 475, 478, 487, 495, 507, 609.

4. The Hague and the Daniel Marot Style

The Hague, or we would have it under its Dutch name of Den Haag, or s'-Gravenhage, is still one of the pleasantest capitals in Europe. But only within the limits of the original village or small town. For the pandemonium of trams and bicycles abates a little under the lofty trees of the Lange Voorhout and along the embattlements of the Vijver. Sixty years ago The Hague must have been a haven of Dutch tranquillity and comfort. But the area of the old city is not so large by half as that of the colleges of Oxford or Cambridge; it is but the extent of the three or four chief London squares, and this is set down in the middle of a huge modern town. The red brick Mauritshuis will be considered by many persons to be the most typical of Dutch private houses, and its note of domesticity will be no more than enhanced when we are told that it was built by Jacob van Campen and Pieter Post for Count Johan Maurits van Nassau, who was Governor of Brazil, and in his troubled times had given serious thought to a scheme for removing the majority of the Dutch population to South America. We will not delay at the Grootekerk, which is the counterpart of many others all over Holland; nor at the more interesting Nieuwekerk, first cousin in style and date to Campen's Westerkerk at Amsterdam, except to notice its curious, star-shaped 'hen-and-chickens' plan, and the carved banks and pulpit of its interior.

Instead, we will penetrate the quiet façades, like those, exactly, of an old London square, in search of Daniel Marot. Certainly, one of the proofs of my own ignorance of Holland, and perhaps the greatest personal discovery of my recent journey, has been the magnificent series of town houses in the Daniel Marot style at The Hague. For now that more research has been done upon them it is wiser and more appropriate to call them by this name, than to attribute them directly to the architect in question. There can be no more splendid examples of the age of the Régence in all Europe. We have to preface our remarks to Englishmen with the statement that this Huguenot artist and craftsman, born in Paris (1650-1718), was chief architect to William III and accompanied him to London, where a surviving relic of his work is the tall, narrow, State Coach of the Speaker of the House of Commons, last seen at the Coronation drawn by its pair of horses, with the silver mace protruding from the window. Daniel Marot, in fact, was something of a universal genius. He painted the walls of staircases, designed furniture and garden vases, left designs for tiles and fabrics, and for ornamental panels, these last much in the manner of Jean Bérain. He laid out gardens, as well as palaces; made drawings for tombs and monuments; drew costumes and scenery for ballets in the approved Baroque style of Juvara and the Bibiena family; while his attention to the smallest details is proved in his interlaced monograms, his engraved door plates, and his varied and beautiful designs for watch cocks. Proofs of Marot's multifarious and versatile activities are continually increasing; to him are due among similar objects the huge blue and white Delft pyramids in the William and Mary part of Hampton Court, eight feet high and designed for the garden display of Dutch flowers, as well as the 14 pagoda tulip or hyacinth vases at Chatsworth, in detachable sections. There are also blue and white milk-pails designed by him at the Victoria and Albert Museum. More of an ornamentalist than architect? But the answer to this question is to be found in the wonderful town houses at The Hague. It is not, however, so simple, for now there appear upon the scene Daniel Marot junior, and Jacob Marot, sons of the great Frenchman, architects of whom little or nothing is known in our language. In the father's will D. Marot is mentioned as painter and J. Marot as architect. Daniel Marot being given as born 1650-5, it was in any event surprising to see these houses of the third or fourth decade of the eighteenth century ascribed to him, for he would be at that time 80 years of age, or more. Yet these white stucco interiors are Régence, not full-fledged Louis xv in manner. We would describe them as belated or retarded French work of 1710-25 in a 1730-40 setting, but it would appear, nevertheless, that they are the work of Daniel Marot senior.

The Royal Library, Lange Voorhout 34, may be the finest of The Hague town houses, and is the work of Marots of the second generation,* having been built in 1734–8 for Adrienne Marguerite Huguetan, widow of Hendrik Carel Graaf van Nassau La Lecq. Its exterior is the typical Marot house; a stone façade with a frontispiece of three storeys and a balustraded roof with a central cresting of heraldry and sculpture. These stone houses, amid so much dark brick, announce their distinct style from the start. The interior of the Royal Library has several good rooms with *boiseries* and mirrors, but it is the white Régence Marot staircase that is its feature, rising up the whole height of the building to the lantern, and with the most splendid stucco carvings. The former German Embassy, now taken over by the Dutch Admiralty, Lange Vijverberg 8, is a little earlier in date, built in 1715 or soon after by Cornelis van Schuylenburch, of a famous old Dutch family, in the lifetime of Daniel Marot senior. The name of an Italian stuccoist, Joh. Baptista Luragho, is preserved in the family archives as having worked here. The staircase is magnificent, once again, with superb wrought iron balusters, but in this instance the feature is the first floor landing, with open lantern above, worked into the richest white Régence interior that could be imagined, with fluted Corinthian pilasters, busts in niches, and most elaborate flowered and figured ceiling.

The search for old houses at The Hague has its improbable moments, as, for instance, the finding of a couple of stucco ceilings, undoubtedly from their early date and character by Daniel Marot senior, in a modern Oriental carpet warehouse at Noordeinde

---

* This is to be assumed; but Daniel Marot worked into his extreme old age, and this house, probably, was built and carried out to his plans.

140. These are so richly and intricately worked that they could be carried out, equally well, as Savonnerie rugs or carpets, being perfect specimens of Louis xiv, not Régence style, and the relics of a house built by Hendrik Fagel (1617-90), first secretary of the States-General. Through a window at the back could be seen the garden pavilion or *tuinkoepel*, with a beautiful interior, lately purchased by H.M. Queen Wilhelmina, and enclosed in the gardens of the Royal Palace. Another, undoubted Marot house, Korte Vijverberg 3, is now a Government office occupied by the Queen's Cabinet or private secretariat, and like Lange Vijverberg 8, was built, originally, by the Schuylenburch family. It has the characteristic white Régence staircase, and other beautiful rooms of later date. But, also, we must not forget to mention the Trèves Zaal, in the Binnenhof, looking out from its long windows over the waters of the Vijver, a great white and gold reception hall built by William iii in 1697 for the States-General. This is one of the most splendid specimens of the Louis xiv style, with no trace of the later Régence, and comparing with the Galerie Dorée of the Hôtel de Toulouse in Paris. The details of the Trèves Saal are remarkably clear and fresh, but for some reason do not reproduce well in a photograph.

Other works by the Marots include the long hall or passage of the Stadhuis; the little Portuguese-Jewish synagogue, now gutted; and the wings of the much damaged Huis ten Bosch. We must recall, also, the palace of Het Loo and its gardens, and, in particular, the painted staircase, there, and at the Huis de Voorst.* Finally, a private house, become a Provincial Library at Middelburg, and now reported as totally destroyed in the recent holocaust of

---

* Funerary monuments by Daniel Marot, not including his rejected designs for a monument to William iii, are to be seen in the Grootekerk at The Hague, and in the village churches of Abcoude, Wyckel, Rhoon, and Heusden. Marot favoured an obelisk as background, in black marble, white marble trophies or escutcheons, and a recumbent figure, generally, in that war-like age, with flags and cannons. We conclude our notice of Marot with a mention of his summer house or *tuinkoepel* at Rozendaal, with *chinoiserie* interior, and many shelves and pedestals for china bowls and jars.

Walcheren, is so much in the style of Marot, and so nearly resembles the town houses at The Hague, with its frontispiece and cresting, that it must be ascribed to him rather than to the Antwerp architect J. P. van Baurscheit, who was concerned in its erection and to whom the credit is given by a leading authority.

But there are other beautiful old houses at The Hague besides those by Daniel Marot and his sons. Some, of course, have gone; 'the two handsome rooms in the style of Louis Quinze'* that were a feature of the Gouvernement van Zuidholland, in the Korte Voorhout, destroyed in the recent war, alas, by the R.A.F.! but understood and forgiven by the patriotic, friendly Dutchmen. Only a few yards away there still stands the graceful, recessed façade, in stone, of the Royal Theatre, formerly the palace of Nassau-Weilburg, a French façade that would not be out of place in Nancy or Bordeaux. The palace of the Queen Mother in the Lange Voorhout, with the gilded lamps and sentry-boxes, is another charming and modest building in French style with fine *boiseries* in the interior, a French house built, by invitation, in a Dutch square. Many old houses, that are now foreign embassies or legations, have good interiors, but of these old houses only one or two are still in private hands. In former times every aristocratic Dutch family had its own house at The Hague, and they lasted, as such, a hundred years later than the rich burgher and merchant houses of Amsterdam, and survived to within living memory. With their passing The Hague has lost, inevitably, much of its especial character.

The Hague has become a mammoth, modern town, with this contradiction that peace and quiet can only be found in its inmost centre. But it is still the political capital of The Netherlands, the seat of Government, and the centre of diplomatic life. Every year,

---

* They were the work of Pieter de Swart (*b.* Rotterdam), who died at The Hague in 1766. He and his pupil, Jacob Bergman, were responsible for most of the fine Louis xv houses at The Hague, those, particularly, with *boiseries*. Jacob Bergman (1730–97) was an able sculptor as well, and 'devoted extreme attention to the decorative portion of the works'. But Pierter de Swart, after Daniel Marot, was best of the architects working at The Hague.

8   *A house in Middelburg*

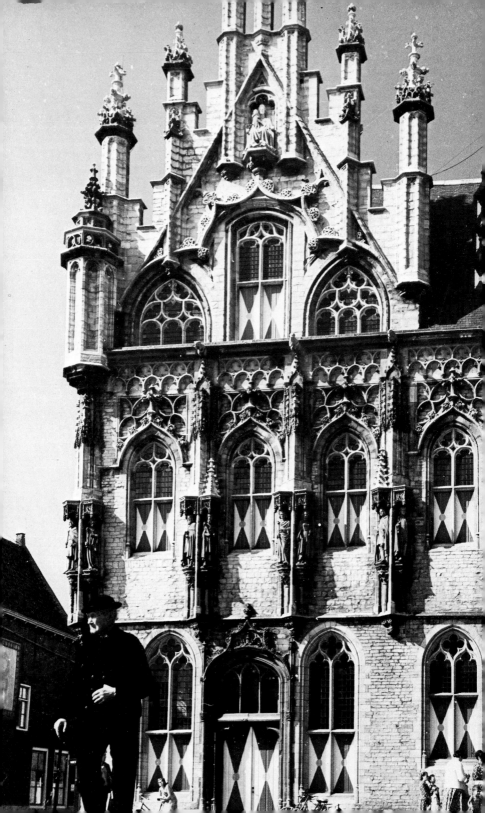

upon the third Tuesday in September, the Queen and the Royal Family drive in state from the palace to the Ridderzaal for the opening of the States-General. Their golden coach, drawn by eight horses, with walking grooms and footmen in the Orange livery, forms a spectacle to be seen, now, in few other capitals but London, and is a relic of the glories of the golden past. But the amateur of seaside towns, in and out of season – and who could be other than that if, like the writer, born and bred in one – cannot omit to pay his compliments to 'the sirens, Metropole and Grand'. The road, through sand dunes and woods of fir trees, sown by the German forces with tank traps and 'dragons' teeth' for the prospective invader from the English coast, leads in a few moments to Scheveningen. Upon a late evening in July I saw it, with the green fires of sunset still incandescent in the bare, North Sea sky. We paced the ghostly promenade, haunted by cheap music, but no one was abroad. We passed hotel after hotel, some still staring with empty windows out to sea, and entered under the disapproving eye of our own countrymen on holiday into the Kurhaus, to listen to the Roumanian Ciganje band. We visited one or more night clubs, and came home late.

Of Scheveningen as the resort of painters we saw nothing. Yet it was famous in its day. But Scheveningen has happy associations for Englishmen. It was here that Charles II embarked in May 1660 for the Restoration, and no reader of Pepys will forget his account of the music and rejoicing. We may know something of the sort again if the red tape is untied and we are liberated from our 'planners'. We did not see the fishermen or fishwives of Scheveningen, a race of whom the French guide remarks that it is 'peu communicatif, et ne montre pas d'empressement pour le baigneur', adding that the costume of the women is 'franchement disgracieux'. But the fishing town still exists, though in new and ugly modern houses, and the square flat-bottomed *boms* are still drawn up on the beach, 'lying', so says de Amicis, but he was a Latin and a romantic, 'one beside the other in a row upon the sand, like the Greek galleys on the shores of Troy'. The costume of the fisherfolk is now nearly extinct, and the fishwives no longer

9 *A cloister in Middelburg*

carry the creels of fish upon their heads, nor take the catch into The Hague in little, low carts drawn by dogs.

Since the above was written in 1947 much additional information on the old houses of The Hague and Amsterdam has come to light. On a recent visit to The Hague in April 1973 I went again to see the ceilings in the carpet warehouse at Noordeinde 12, and was then reminded of the beautiful pavilion or tea-house lying behind this building, but the information came too late to be able to see it. This, too, is ascribed hopefully to Daniel Marot and may be one of the prettiest old buildings in The Hague. We did however, after trying some four different entrances on two successive days at various times on both days – for all four entrances were opposite more or less to our hotel – contrive to enter the 'underground' Old Catholic Church at Molenstraat 38, the very existence of which in compliance with conditions imposed by the municipal authorities when building began in 1722, is certainly invisible from the street, 'et qui n'est pas sans évoquer le style de Daniel Marot' (*Guide Bleu* : Benelux).

Even so little as 25 years ago it seemed unlikely that Daniel Marot, even with two sons to help him, could have accomplished all that he is given credit for, at The Hague, in Amsterdam, and at Het Loo and other châteaux in the Country. This is, therefore, the moment to summarize what Dutch savants have discovered for themselves about the continuation of this late Regency style in eighteenth-century Holland, in the course of which the names of forgotten sculptors and architects have come to light. Such, then, is the explanation for the extraordinary quantity and quality of old houses in the two towns mentioned, in Rotterdam before its wilful destruction by the Nazis, and in Utrecht, Middelburg, and other old towns. To quote an article by Pieter Fischer in *Apollo* (November 1972) : 'two artists who until recently were little more than names and who are still frequently confused with each other – Ignatius van Logteren (1685-1732) – and his son Jan van Logteren (1709-1745) – have come to the fore in late years. . . . They are among the artists who contributed most to the appearance of the famous Amsterdam canals with their patrician houses. To the son, in particular, who had such a short life, is ascribed the beautiful stuccowork busts, statues in *alto relievo* and balconies with musicians, on the stair of Heerengracht 475, taken hitherto for the very epitome of the Daniel Marot style, and as well the more Rococo interior at Heerengracht 168.'

Artists 'who inherited the van Logteren's exquisite qualities', according to this same authority, were Michael Schee or Shee (1697–1739) and the De Wildes, Bernardus and Thijs or Mathijs, 'maybe brothers?' the very uncertainty in the spelling of their names showing how little, up to date, is known about them. Was for instance Samuel Wilde (1747–1832), the foremost painter of theatre pieces after Zoffany, some relative of the Dutch de Wildes? A beautiful white marble chimney piece and overmantel of Venus and Vulcan by the de Wilde brothers, from a house in Heerengracht, is now in the Carnegie Institute of Art at Pittsburgh, U.S.A. and shows the Dutch Rococo at its height of grace and elegance. The names of other sculptors and architects are given who worked at Utrecht and at country houses along the River Vecht, with still others active at Haarlem, Leeuwarden and Groningen, but this little-known territory of the arts is illustrated in the last sentence of the article from which we are quoting. It ends: 'the Dutch eighteenth century came to an agreeable and satisfying conclusion with the work of men such as Ziesenis, Swart and Van der Wall.'

5. The Waterland and Noord Holland

*'Pray tell me for what purpose are such galligaskins as
the Dutch burthen themselves with contrived, but to
tuck up a flouncing tail and thus cloak the deformity of
a dolphin-like termination?'* – WILLIAM BECKFORD.

Let us begin this chapter at 'the Arcadia of Zaanland', the villages
in question being Koog aan de Zaan and Krommenie, just beyond Zaandam, which is fascinating in itself with its painted
wooden houses, and about 10 or 12 miles, not more, from Amsterdam. The little houses in the two villages, or they are hardly
more than cabins, are not in the 'florid cockney' style a nineteenth-
century traveller ascribes to Broek. It may be that we should have
found much to admire at Broek-in-Waterland; that the gardens
of Mijnheeren Van der Beck and Bakker were but late accretions;
and that many of the houses, far from exhibiting 'a caricature of
Dutch manners', were exceedingly light and graceful, and indeed,
'Arcadian'. For such is the truth at Koog aan de Zaan and
Krommenie, at both of which villages a house or two is still standing in bucolic Rococo, houses of a brick ground floor with but an
upper window, and the gable or upper part all wooden, painted
red or green, and with roofs 'glittering in the sun with polished
tiles of different colours'. The little Molenmuseum* in the former
village, with no other ornament but a pair of simple pillared
doorways, is remarkable for its delightful frontispiece achieved,
merely, by masking the two middle windows with a white wooden

* The only museum in the world dedicated to windmills.

urn and wreaths of flowers and putting a mirror frame, it is
no more than that, around the upper window. An invention
simple enough, and in bucolic style, but when we look at the
grace of its shell or feather cresting, and at the double wreath
or swag below, and then at the side gable, and realize that it is no
larger than a modern bungalow, we could wish that photographs
of these little houses were in the hands, and brains, of our housing
authorities and planners. Another of the Koog aan de Zaan houses
is more simple and delightful, still, with its board gable framed in
Rococo, and ornamented upper windows, a gable like a plain
ship or barge front, and a style accomplished in entire simplicity
of means. Yet Krommenie, we could almost say, is even prettier; a
house, Zuiderhoofdstraat 115, no bigger than the smallest cottage,
but with 'Arcadian' gable, model swags and pilasters, a little later
in date, it must be Louis xvi, urns, more wreaths, and little sculptured panels; another, Noorderhoofdstraat 74, more imposing
dated, in compliance with our suggestion, 1786, and more
elaborate in whorl and pilaster and cornucopia, but with façade
of a doorway and two windows, only; finally, Zuiderhoofdstraat
65, last address in Krommenie, a shagreen cottage of pink brick
and mortar, with a gable and ornamented upper window, weather
boarding behind, as with these other houses, and exhibiting, not a
caricature of anything, but a model of how an Arcadia can be
made of two-roomed cottages. We must think otherwise of Dutch
manners and cleanliness after this, our first introduction to
Arcadian Holland. All that is missing is the Dutch costume, which
is not far away.

By now, we are nearing the Waterland. But, first, we come to
Monnikendam and Edam. At Monnikendam there is a fine old
brick church and a main street of old brick houses, some with
mediaeval fronts, others with the mirror backs. The Stadhuis,
first of the Town Halls, is in a patrician house of 1760, a building
of three storeys with copious Rococo coat-of-arms and cresting,
iron stair rail taking the form of a twisting sea serpent, an entrance
hall and corridor with good stuccowork, and a room with painted
leather hangings in the floral, Chinese manner. Here and there, in

front of the houses, are wrought iron guards or rails of peculiar Dutch form, often like an arc of a circle. Altogether, Monnikendam is an exceedingly charming little town, and it must have much else like the *bombé* Rococo stair and pulpit of the Evangelical-Lutheran church, which I missed. We have the sense that we are in a little world apart, and that the inhabitants need go no more than once or twice in their lives to Amsterdam. Yet Monnikendam with its eel and herring fisheries is not 10 miles from the capital.

The road from Monnikendam to Edam, still more from any one village in the Waterland to another, becomes, both at the moment and in retrospect, like a whole morning or an afternoon spent upon the journey. The distance may be three miles, not more. I have crossed the Sahara from Marrakesh to Leptis Magna, and its stages from oasis to oasis do not stand out, in memory, as being further. It is because of the polders. The clock runs at another pace in the green water-meadows, below the winding dykes. The steeple of the next church, three miles away, becomes the symbol of a metropolis which you see, far off, and may visit in a fortnight's time. It is the tempo of the old Dutch painters, and except for Hals and Rembrandt, the tempo of them all, which is their charm. Perhaps it lends an exaggerated importance to what lies near to hand. The especial light, the *gris clair* loved of painters, for there must be reasons or aptitudes to explain the presence of such a host of painters in a small land? We do not know. But, certainly, this is the excuse for their bright interiors and fantastic costumes. An excuse of a sort, but not enough, for it does not explain why or how the extraordinary communities whom we shall visit have come to be besieged within themselves. Nevertheless, it is a question of tempo. It is the only reason for it all; for the golden helmets of the Frisian women; for the Bibles of Staphorst that the women carry to church upon silver chains; for the glazed chintz cuirasses of Spakenburg, another fishing village; the 'Indian' stuffs of Hindeloopen; the hundred and one wonders of Zeeland and Friesland, which two provinces formed the 'paradise' of the farmer and rich peasant. The secret of it all is isolation and a quiet life, and in the monotony of grey sea and green meadows their costumes and adornments were so many drags or weights on Time.

But insensibly, as on all such journeys, we have drawn nearer our next stopping place. We are at Edam. In its streets of mediaeval houses we see the women walking, or standing in the doorways, whom we noticed from the windows of the restaurant, miles away – it is only 12 miles! – in Amsterdam. They are the same tribe of women; but they are the first ones whom we see, and we are only upon the confines of the Waterland. These are not in gala costume; they are in mere working clothes, but they have the long dark skirts touching upon the pavement and a horned or peaked cap. Not peasants, but women in some mediaeval harbour town. Edam may be distant, now, but how remote it must have been! And we would like to have seen it in the time of the trio of freaks, or worthies of Edam, of whom there are portraits in the little museum; Tryntje Kester, the 'Great Maid', a skipper's daughter, and 12 feet in height at 17, if we believe it; Pieter Dirksz, the Burgomaster, with red forked beard so long that it trails on the ground but the ends of it can be gathered and held up in his arms; the third freak being an immense, fat innkeeper. We would like to have seen the three worthies in their pews in church, and what a beautiful church it is, with a lovely quiet interior; good Renaissance windows given by other Dutch towns, only inferior to the painted glass at Gouda; brass 'octopus' chandeliers; pews and 'banks' innumerable on which to seat, in imagination, the Burgomaster, fat innkeeper, and skipper's daughter; and high up, under the roof, one of the terrifying 'rat walks' which are contrived by the Dutch in their churches so that even the roof beams may be dusted!

But Edam has a Stadhuis which is a gem of Dutch architecture, and which possesses to our mind all the architectural quality of Holland. A little red brick building with white wooden cupola, built in 1737, and its fine red brick apart, it has no other feature but one of the most beautiful and elaborate of overdoors. But the whole building is so sensible and solid, and in no hurry. It is, indeed, a late arrival in a tradition that, already, was upwards of 100 years old, a child born to middle-aged parents and intelligent, as those are reputed to be, but more solid and sensible than pretty. Such is the outward appearance of the Town Hall of Edam, but, within, it gives rein to fantasy. The only hint of that lay in the rich over-door and lantern, or perhaps in the crest of a bull above the upper window. The entrance hall, the staircase and first floor landing, are panelled in white stucco, heavy and exuberant, but work of the abstract order without figures. But it is the Court Room, on the left, that is our first introduction into this little new world that we would fain discover, a world as delightful as it is unrecorded, for it is not mentioned, this is the beauty of it, in any guide book. We shall find that the painted Court Rooms in the Town Halls are among the most fanciful of decorations in the whole of Holland, and we have them to ourselves, for no one else has written of them. The Court Room at Edam is painted with the Judgment of Solomon by W. Rave, an unknown painter, working in a manner that we would describe as Veronese, at many removes, but come to rest among the dairy lands and polders. It has not the elegance of the painted Court Rooms at Sneek and Dokkum, the Friesland Court Rooms, nor that of Goes in Zeeland, all of which are works of a high order by any standard, and by that much the more entrancing because ignored, utterly, and forgotten in their bucolic setting.

At Edam it is the green and gold decorations which are so charming; the carved mantelpiece, the green and gold chairs of the justices and lawyers, above all, the green and gold carved rail behind which stood the prisoners, arraigned for what offences? Imagination can only answer for contraventions in milk, cheese, or butter. We can think of no serious crimes being tried, here, in this 'Arcadian' Court Room. We can picture to ourselves the Burgomaster in his huge wig, and the other bigwigs whom we would see in their 'banks' and pulpits in the great church. The prisoners, also, must have been most curious in their clumsy shoes and baggy breeches. But as a room in green and gold, for any purpose, this is not far behind the green and gold card room in the

Schloss at Würzburg, if that still exists. The ceiling is plain. But another detail; the board floor is sanded and the edges of this round the walls are brushed, as it were, with a wave pattern. Those wavy lines are in contrast to the plain grain of the floor boards, enough to remind someone, much travelled, of the sand gardens of Kyoto, this sand we like to think, being of the sort referred to in an old book, where, writing of Zaandam and the country round, it says, 'In some of the windmills a peculiar kind of sandstone brought from the neighbourhood of Bremen is reduced into dust solely to furnish the Dutch housewife with sand for her floor.' It must have been upon raked sand, of the self-same origin, that the offending cherry stones were found that caused a riot, long ago, at Broek-in-Waterland.

A glorious figure is coming towards us down one of the narrow streets of Haarlem, a glorious but, withal, forbidding figure who positively makes a noise as he is walking. It is because of the swish of his clothes, and he comes so near that we could stretch out a hand and touch him. Maybe the red brick houses make him more gorgeous in his doublet and black breeches.

A tall young man with curly, sandy hair, clean shaven, with a flushed red face and big, aquiline nose, who looks at us intently, and disdainfully, as he hurries by. Where have we heard this noise before, of hose and doublet? Only with the Swiss Guard at the Vatican. But here are no black, yellow, and red stripes, nor halberds; no colonnades, nor rainbow fountains. Instead, it is a town of red brick houses. We look at his black shoes upon the pale brick of the pavement, and then from the uncompromising, the even insolent stare of this black musketeer or archer with the sandy hair, to his high black hat, more suited, we would have said, to a Spanish lady, but then we remember that the Madrileñas or the Sevillañas wore snoods or mantillas; they would never venture in the streets in hats like his. It is a tall hat with a brim; with a black plume and a white plume, and a knotted cord placed half-way up the crown; the hat of an ensign or lieutenant in some company or regiment. This hat is balanced in extravagance by his ruff, which is of the richest starched lace, and he wears a black silk doublet that is sleeveless like a waistcoat. It is this that gives him the air of an officer, a hussar on foot, and at once a halberdier and banner bearer, but without the halberd. His sleeve is of a lighter, tabbied stuff that is flecked with marks or tails, and his gloved hand has a laced fringe. He has full black breeches of the same stuff as his doublet, and black stockings, the black silk shines with the white lights in it; but this black peacock of an officer has, also, a sword hanging at his side with a great golden pommel, a pommel with an openwork guard of gilt steel, while his sword sash is gorgeous with embroidery and his baldric is of embroidered leather. Now and again he rests his hand upon his sword hilt, but more often his gloved hand is upon his hip, and in any case the blade in its scabbard, to speak truly, does not hang at his side, he carries it horizontally to the ground, where it is held up half-way down his black silk breeches. But this is not all. A red and white silk sash falls from one shoulder and is tied in a bow upon his other hip, and upon the same shoulder he has a heavy white, and red, and orange banner.

Where is he hurrying to? He passes us, and has to bow his head under the low brick archway and pull his banner after him. And we follow, noticing that white, and red, and orange flags are hung out in the street. There is the sound of shouting, singing, roaring, and we find ourselves in a large room across a courtyard, with a gargantuan banquet laid out upon a table, great goblets of wine, and huge pewter dishes full of oysters. It is the Banquet of Officers of the St Joris-Doelen and the Cloveniers-Doelen (Archers or Arquebusiers of St George and St Andrew), both companies together, of the Civic Guard of Haarlem. The hall is full of burghers of all ages up to 55 or 60, in huge black sombreros and stiff white ruffs that differ according to the wearer, for they are articles of dress that take on the individuality of their owners, and are as personal as handwriting.

Ruffs of all descriptions, for fashions change, but you can tell from his ruff who is boasting or vainglorious, who is careful living and religious, or who is a bore. There are the creamy ruffs, those that circumscribe the neck, and nothing more. In the case of these, the sombrero becomes Dutch and not Spanish, by reason, not of the owner's features, but of the manner in which he wears the sombrero and makes it into the black hat of the Puritan, the black hat of Praise God Barebones and of Hogarth's plates for *Hudibras,* the black hat worn by Dunkers and Amish, even now, among the Pennsylvania Dutch settlers. But others of the sombreros have light blue or orange feathers. There are ruffs that are like a starched and foaming ballet skirt and, by that, the more incongruous round a drinker's face. The more aristocratic of the company wear the lace collar of the Cavalier. And we notice a pair of Arquebusiers, particularly, because they are standing near together and are so alike in feature, with fair hair and moustaches, and little pointed beards, in Cavalier hats both of them, one with a lace collar and little tassels, a light blue sash round his waist, and the other, who leans both hands upon a stick, in a great orange sash wound twice around him. Next to them, a Cavalier in a yellow or buff uniform holds his staff or baton in one hand and has a wonderful light blue silk sash, looped in a bow, and with deep fringed ends. The Arquebusiers of St Andrew are richest of all for the intricacy of their sword hilts and the colour of their silk sashes. Those in black doublets have white, light blue, or orange sashes, painted to a miracle, while a man, standing, in a yellow-grey doublet, has a miraculous pale blue scarf or sash tied in an enormous bow. And there are cuffs as well as ruffs. An Arquebusier with sandy hair and beard, hatless, in a black doublet, who sits talking, his collar, sleeve, and silk sash painted to such a likeness of a living person that it is almost embarrassing to make remarks about him. And there is an older man, stick in hand, the other hand upon his hip, who sits looking out of the picture, as though not approving, but wishing, at the same time, to be the one serious person in the painting.

For, by now, there is scarce one sober man amongst them. The Arquebusiers of St George wear yellow silk scarves. One of them, with his white, and red, and orange banner furled upon his shoulder, with ruffled hair, stands up to leave the table, and holds his black hat in his other. His black coat, with the lights upon it, is a wonderful passage of painting. But the man sitting next to him, who has turned round in his chair to look at us, is, indeed, one of the marvels of the painter's hand. It is not only his ruffled, dark hair and the half-drunken excitement in his eyes (he is the same Cavalier, in buff coat, baton in hand, whom we mentioned in another of the paintings) but it is the virtuosity of the buffalo-skin jerkin that he is wearing, and more than all else the sheer bravado of his sleeve and elbow raised towards us as he turns down his wine glass, and we see, through the rim of it, part of the pewter dish of oysters upon which the hand of another man, behind him, who also looks at us, squeezes his half-lemon. In point of technique this episode is one of the supreme passages in painting, being only matched in brushwork by passages in Velásquez or in Manet. The figures, however, most nearly resemble the sculptured portraits by Bernini. An extraordinary vitality of effect, as in Bernini, is produced by apparently simple means. The whole picture is ablaze with the yellow scarves or sashes. In all of the five Civic Guard groups of Frans Hals the colour motifs are of this simple or straightforward character; yellow silk scarves in this instance, the St George group of 1627, which is his masterpiece; but, in the others, it is the doublets, sashes, feathers, of light blue, orange, violet; in all of them, the black or buff uniforms of the Arquebusiers with their yellow, blue or salmon scarves; and in all, the red, and white, and orange banners. It is the virtuosity of rendering which makes them into a painter's miracle. This, but above all, the instantaneity of vision. The Doelen groups, meetings or banquets of Civic Guards, offered the greatest opportunity open to Dutch painters.* Rembrandt's *Night Watch* is to be numbered

---

* There were, also, the 'Regent' pictures, groups of the Governors of hospitals and charities. Three of these are included in the eight master-pieces of Frans Hals at Haarlem; the *Regenten* of the Elizabeth Hospital, and the groups of the *Regenten* and *Regentessen*, Governors and Women Governors of the Old Men's Almshouse, the last paintings of Hals, done when he was 80 years old. Rembrandt's *Anatomy Lesson*, in the Mauritshuis, is a 'Regent' picture; and other painters of these subjects include van Mierevelt, and Thomas de Keyser, son of the architect of the Westerkerk at Amsterdam, and brother-in-law of our English sculptor Nicholas Stone.

with these; and also the 'Doelen' groups of Govert Flinck and of Bartholomew van der Helst, the latter much admired by Reynolds, who wrote of one of his paintings, in the Rijksmuseum, that 'Perhaps this is the finest picture of portraits in the world'. None, by any other hand, possess the instantaneous, flashlight grouping of Frans Hals.

His is the most life-like rendering of the Dutchmen of his time, so like the living persons that it is impossible to understand the poverty and degradation of his career. Hals was sued, repeatedly, for rent, and even for shoes, and for his baker's bill. He borrowed money from the baker. He pawned his belongings. He could not earn enough to keep himself alive. He was a heavy drinker. It may even be that he was mentally unstable. But never has there been such a hand in painting, and this was his undoing. The figures rise up at us out of his groups of archers. Four or five of the faces become so well known to us that we remember them in the middle of the night and wonder where we met them. If it is living Dutchmen of the golden age of Holland (in the lifetime of Shakespeare) that we would know, here is our opportunity, and we have taken it in the brick streets of Haarlem on our way to Alkmaar and Hoorn. For there is no better way to understand the dead cities of the Zuyder Zee, and to people them with living persons.

Alkmaar, it is true, has been spoiled by riches. In the result, it is a livelier place to live in than the dead cities, proper. And it is not upon the Zuyder Zee, but inland, in the middle of North Holland, in midst of all the pastures. They lie for 10 or 15 miles in every direction from the North Sea to the Zuyder Zee, and from the North Sea Canal to the Isle of Texel. This wealth comes into the town in market carts on Thursday nights, or early upon Friday morning. To lovers of farm wagons these are not so interesting as the hooded carts of Walcheren, that come to the Middelburg market, but the carts of North Holland are painted blue inside, and they are loaded with the red or yellow globes of cheeses. Others come by canal; an arrival which is in rustic parody to the oranges and melons that are brought by barge to Venice. For the cheeses look like oranges or great citrus fruits; or are they more like huge puff balls or funguses found growing on the grassy meadows? They are handled by cheese porters in white linen uniforms with comical straw hats, each with the coloured ribbon of his guild to match the colour of his hand barrow; bucolics who, with their blunt-ended boots and abbreviated 'pants' or trousers, with the motions, too, of their throwing and catching the round cheeses, resemble the yokels in a ballet. Do the cheeses travel as far as Alkmaar that are made in the Isle of Texel, 'green' cheeses of much local renown, made from ewes milk, and that are given their particular flavour by the ewes droppings which are put in a linen bag and steeped in the milk? We hope not. The northern extremity of that grassy island, we digress, with its flocks of sheep in tens of thousands, is called Eierland, 'land of eggs', from the sea birds that come from Norway to lay their eggs there. But we return to Alkmaar, where there is not much more to see. The usual Dutch church, with a model of a man-of-war in full sail given by a seaman under de Ruyter; but the dullness of the streets is redeemed by the cake shops and confectioners, even though the chocolates are dummy chocolates, and by the flower market full of spikes of gladiolas, when I saw it, in all shades and undertones of rose and pink, down by a corner of the canal, for the flowers, too, are brought by barge. But, also, Alkmaar has one or two good buildings, a private house, 'Het Moriaenshoofd' in the main street, now, lamentably, the Municipal Archives, a house built of stone, which is rare in Holland, with a terrific Baroque cresting of a Minerva? lance in hand, and another allegorical figure, with an eagle between, and below, an elaborate bas-relief of several figures. The hall corridor is richly worked in stucco, and there is a painted room that would be a sensation among amateurs of the fine arts in England, or indeed in any country but Holland, where the surpassing wealth of their one great century has blinded them to that which followed. This painted room, with its gardens and landscapes and ornamental swans, could be by the hand of Dirk Dalens or of Isaac de Moucheron, old 'Ordonnance' as we prefer to call him, by one of the authors of the painted rooms in Amsterdam; but it is as likely to be by some other painter of whom we have never heard before.

And upon a canal on the outskirts of Alkmaar there is an alms-house, the Provenhofje van Wildeman, a building of 1714 with a high central body of two floors, a statue of Hercules, club on shoulder, the 'savage' or 'wild man' in a niche with shell background over the door, smaller statues on the pediment to either side, and a garden at the back, of pollard trees with more broken statues.

A dozen miles away over the polders lies the ancient town of Hoorn. The way leads across the Schermer and the Beemster polders, which is to say, across the lands of cheese and butter, though it must be more beautiful to arrive at Hoorn by sea. There is a Harbour Tower in Dutch Renaissance, with pagoda bell tower added that, like the West Gate, is the sort of building admired by many persons for not much other reason than that it is genuine and old. Nevertheless, there should be much to anticipate from this old city. Here are its sons: Willem Schouten who doubled South America and called the stormy promontory Cape Hoorn; Tasman who discovered Tasmania and New Zealand; and Coen (of no ulterior import) who founded the Dutch dominions in the East Indies.* All these from a small town. But it had, then, 60,000 inhabitants, and many of the ships and sailors of Tromp came from Hoorn. It was not a dead town, as it is today, but alive with such characters, or their betters, as we have admired in the groups of the Civic Guards by Hals, at Haarlem. The long streets of old houses could not be more picturesque. They lean towards each other at every angle, many of them being as much out of the perpendicular as the leaning towers of Bologna. The only other streets of such slanting houses known to me are in certain towns in France, but those are timber or half-timber buildings. These are of the universal brick. Many are beautiful; one particularly, of later date, that has a white swan riding in Rococo reeds and waters on a wooden fanlight or overdoor. Hoorn, moreover, is the town in Holland that has most sculptured panels upon the outsides of the houses. There is a bas-relief upon one house of the naval battle of

* The possessive, learned columns of the *Jewish Encyclopaedia* do not decide upon this point, but would like to claim him.

the Zuyder Zee, the defeat of the Spanish Stadthouder de Bossu, and attendant winds in the shape of naked women holding sails or wind scarves in the pose of skipping ropes. It was from the top-floor window of this house that the battle was best seen, continuing all day and night till the Spaniard surrendered on board his galleon, *The Inquisition.** This same naval action is commemorated by a big painting, in a stupendous carved frame of wood with drums and oars and trumpets at the Stadhuis, a picture that hangs over the mantelpiece in a fine late eighteenth-century room with good panelling and wall lights, late Louis XVI in style, an indescribable dark olive-green in colour, and the more surprising by its tardy accomplishment at a town so defunct and old as Hoorn.†

But Enkhuizen, another old 'dead' town a few miles away, is not less full of beautiful buildings of all periods. Upon the way to it the road passed by some bulb fields that give a hint of what

---

* Compare the Soviet habit of calling their big battleships, the *Danton, Marat, Robespierre*, or by Revolutionary dates, *17 October, 1 March*, and so forth. The majority of seamen of all ranks, in spite of this, might prefer to serve on board a *Charlotte Corday*, or better still, an *Emma Hamilton*.

† *The National Costumes of Holland* tells us that Hoorn was the centre of Dutch trade with the East Indies, and that the costumes of the wives of the burghers and rich cattle farmers of the neighbourhood showed East Indian influence. A coloured plate is given of a top-hatted old gentleman in a lovely waistcoat of pale blue and silver damask, and dark blue suit with great silver cartwheel buttons. His wife, or daughter, has a lace cap with beautiful gold head ornaments and her skirt is of purple red damask with a design of red flowers upon it. The skirts of Hoorn and its neighbourhood were especially beautiful, often in shades of blue and green or embroidered in bright colours on a white linen ground. In contrast, upon another plate we are shown the costumes of Bergen-Binnen, close by, but upon the North Sea. The man wears a wedding waistcoat, with sleeves of damask with woven pattern of black, green, yellow, red, and blue flowers, of Persian aspect; while the woman has a close hood, as in Holbein's portrait of Anne of Cleves, but her skirt, worn over five or six petticoats, is of blue damask with an eighteenth-century flower pattern woven in a silvery grey. The old 'dead' towns are dead no longer when we can think of them with such flowered skirts and waistcoats of Persian and East Indian pattern, and with Holbein women reappearing, two centuries later, in pale blue and silver dresses.

10   Dordrecht

11   Amstel House, near Amsterdam

the neighbourhood of Haarlem must be in the full flowering season. It may be that the suggestion flatters, for the nurseries outside Enkhuizen are not so regular in row, there are not the platoons of tulips or hyacinths. The effect at Enkhuizen was softer and less staring, they were fields of ranunculuses when I passed by, a flower in sad decline from its heyday when 600 or 800 named varieties were grown by the French and Dutch florists, a flower that, like the tulip, was loved by the Turks, who fancied they could see in it a resemblance to their striped turbans. The ranunculus and the cornflower made a soft haze on the outskirts of Enkhuizen, made it unnecessary, too, to go off into ecstasies about the Dromedary Tower that, in truth, is anything but beautiful. The Stadhuis, a stone house of 1688, has a good plain exterior with balcony, and the Burgomaster's room is adorned with wall paintings by Romeyn de Hooghe, not of any particular merit, but interesting because of the hand that painted them, for de Hooghe, a nephew of the artist, was the foremost book illustrator of the seventeenth century.* His drawings for the *Fables* of La Fontaine are famous; and he made the marvellous illustrations, using that term in its proper sense, for *Les Indes Orientales et Occidentales* (1680), a work that in the generous comprehension of its title is an exact reflection of the poetical haze or distance with which it dealt. Java, Sumatra, Borneo, Bali, Celebes, and the Moluccas are included; also the Americas. His engravings for this great feat of the imagination had much effect upon the design of tapestries for such series as *Les Indes Galantes;* upon the figures on early Meissen porcelain; and upon those on lacquer cabinets. It was curious and most unexpected to find his wall paintings, of which I had read no warning, at Enkhuizen. There is, also, a splendid eighteenth-century building, the Snouck van Loosen Institution, for what that name may portend, and this, again, no guide book has thought fit to mention. This house must date from about 1760. The stone exterior is of pavilion height and shape, with good iron railing in the angles, and a rich stone coping with urns and coats of arms. The

* The relationship of Romeyn de Hooghe and Pieter de Hooch is disputed by Dutch authorities.

entrance hall or corridor is long and narrow with overdoors of reclining figures in deep stucco relief, Mars in one panel, Venus in
another, the latter, a Dutch-looking maiden sitting upright in the
bulrushes and holding what is, obviously, her flaxen hair in a
free hand. The plaster ceiling to this corridor is of fine pattern.
What was formerly the dining-room has walls of painted leather
and a good Rococo frame over the mantelpiece, while the draw-
ing-room has an overmantel in outrageous Rococo, figures of
Cupids with dolphin tails, *chinoiserie* birds, another Cupid with
an arrow, a riot of scrolls and foliage, and to either side of the fireplace most charming Rococo shelves or glassless cabinets, meant
for china. This house, too, one of the most delightful of its kind
in Holland, was a surprise to find in Enkhuizen.*

We will let Medemblik be the last of the decaying towns. It has
little or nothing, but these two things, the door of its Orphanage
or Burgerweeshuis, and the tomb or grave slab of Lord George
Murray. The first is but a door up a flight of a few steps, but the
wooden panelling of the door itself, in two compartments, is of
the richest and most balanced Rococo, lovely 'Chippendale'
panels, they could be, of fantastic carving, with an overdoor
above, in white wood, which is a little masterpiece of fantasy. And
the grave slab? This is in memory of Lord George Murray (he is
buried outside the church), who commanded for the Young
Chevalier at Prestonpans, upon the march to Derby, and on the
fatal day of Culloden. He died here in exile in 1760. How lonely
he must have felt in this old, decaying town! Was he buried, we
wonder, in a tartan plaid? What can have been his life at
Medemblik? Was there a friend's house in which he could go to

* Locke, on his visit to Holland between 1685–9, a sort of religious
sightseeing tour, for his object was to search out the different sects of
Dutch dissenters, wrote of Enkhuizen as the commercial rival to Amsterdam. 'From Hoorn to Enkhuizen,' he writes, 'a distance of ten miles, the
way is all pitched with clinkers and beset with boors' houses – almost, as it
were, one street. The houses are of a pretty, odd fashion, the barn joining
to the dwelling house making a part of it. Enkhuizen has a fair East India
house, the most handsome and stately of anything in the town.' It was in
this Oriental depot that the mariners of Hindeloopen, *vide post* pp. 107–116,
bought chintzes and Indian cottons for their wives.

dine? Had he a Scots servant with him, or was he quite alone? And for a long while after leaving Medemblik, while feeling thankful not to have to sleep a night there, we find the picture of the lonely exile banishes other images of the dead cities of the Zuyder Zee.

6. Friesland

We are drawing near to what, not only to ourselves but to many other persons, is a new and undiscovered land on the far side of the Zuyder Zee. For another country with its own language lies within Holland. Not a Wales or Brittany, nothing rough, nor mountainous. But Friesland is the country, particularly, of costumes, of peasants or farmers, and religious sects, something of a pastoral kingdom or land apart, another country, we would call it, in the kingdom of Cockaigne. There is nothing much else to think of while we wait for Friesland and wonder what we shall see there. For at the moment Noord Holland still stretches endlessly into the distance, and the only sign that we are coming near to the end of it is a low grass embankment, no higher than a railway cutting, that we know must be the dyke. If only we could look over the top of it we should see the Zuyder Zee.

Round here for many miles it was flooded by the Germans. The waters reached up to the first floor of the houses. You can still see the high-water mark above the ground floor windows, and many house walls were crushed entirely by the weight of waters. It is a sinister and horrible reminder of how much the Dutch have suffered in many parts of Holland, for this entire district is like a treeless desert. By now, on the July evening when we saw it after a long day of Alkmaar, Hoorn, and Enkhuizen, the sun was beginning to decline, and it produced a feeling of uneasiness as to what would be this new country of Friesland that we were approaching, mixed, also, with apprehension as to what sort of an hotel we should find ourselves sleeping at for the night. It was getting cold and chilly, though there was still an hour or more of light.

Part of the excitement of going to Friesland is that it is reached by a causeway, over the great dyke that seals the entrance to the Zuyder Zee. It is like the approach to Venice, but 10 times as long, and takes twenty minutes, in a fast motor car, along a road that is perfectly flat and straight, stretching out of sight in either direction when you are half-way down its length, banked up on the outer side into a long rampart of grass and loose stones, with a view to the near side over an eternity of shallow waters, with long, low islands in the distance that are little more than shoals or mud banks, and a fishing boat, here and there, as the only sign of life. It was over this causeway that the retreating Germans came pouring in an endless column, when the war ended, trying to get back to Germany by foot. But this causeway from North Holland to Friesland, though not often mentioned as such, is among the great engineering feats of modern times. At either end there are huge pumping stations to regulate the level of the waters. Apart from that, no other building in sight but a restaurant in a cement tower, at about half-way, no frontier guard, nor customs post, nothing to announce the journey from one language to another, and that we are arriving in a strange land. The metalled road is so flat and level that in this July weather mirages play along its surface. After a long while, when you imagine you have come to the end of it, when a miserable islet which is nothing more than a patch of stunted grass has been left far behind, the causeway begins again and continues till you reach the complicated machinery of another pumping station, then drops below the level of one more dyke and we have arrived in Friesland, and after a run of another half-hour through the twilight we arrive late, but in time for dinner, at Leeuwarden, to wake up in this new country upon a radiant morning.

The plan of Leeuwarden, the capital of Friesland, shows a city surrounded by the waters of one canal and intersected by another. It is, thus, a water town as much, or nearly so, as any other town in Holland. The illusion that we are in a separate little country is supported by its history, for Friesland had a Stadthouder to itself and a separate administration, the first to hold office being John of Nassau, brother to William the Silent, a prince of decidedly philoprogenitive tendencies, for he married three times and had 25 children. The office was made hereditary for his descendants in 1674, and so continued until John William Friso was elected Stadthouder of the seven United Provinces in 1717, the present House of Orange being descended from this prince of Friesland. This later history, which rather resembles that of some little German principality, is redeemed from dullness by the early history of the Frisians, and by their continuing character of independence. This race was never conquered by the Romans. It is not that, like the Irish, they were never invaded by the legions, but that they defeated them in battle, as a result of which the Auricomi of Tacitus, defined vaguely by Ptolemy the geographer as inhabiting the Cimbrian Chersonese or in fact Denmark, began a Roman fashion. Their 'flaming red hair and green eyes' became the rage, and the Emperor Antoninus 'did not hesitate to sacrifice himself to the mode of the day, and covered his head with blond perruque'. Something is wrong. For the Frisians are not noted for red hair and green eyes. The women are famous for their blue eyes and *cheveux de lin* or ash-blonde hair. This, above all, is the distinctive appearance of their race, and they are to be known by it wherever seen in Holland. As to their inhabiting Denmark, there is more of truth in that. The population of all the Frisian Islands, Dutch and German, are of Frisian origin. This included Heligoland and the North Frisian isles as far as the sandy bar of Sylt, an island 30 miles long and in most places only half a mile in width, which was Danish until 1863 when Schleswig was taken from the Danes. Whether the inhabitants of Jutland are of the same origin I have been unable to discover. Should this be so, the Varangian Guard of the Byzantine Emperors, who were recruited from the Danes of Thyland, or Thule, in the dunes of Jutland, were Frisians. The language of the Frisians is said to nearly resemble 'broad' Yorkshire and to be intelligible to York-

shire fishermen.* It is, at any rate, not understood by other Dutchmen, and it cannot, therefore, be similar to Flemish, which is a
difference more of accent than of vocabulary, and can be read
and spoken by most Dutchmen. Nor, clearly, does it resemble
German. We like to think of it, ourselves, as the true 'double-
Dutch' of English legend, for Dutch, in itself, is difficult enough
for an Englishman to understand, while the fact that here in
Holland there is another and separate language, of the existence
of which many Englishmen are not aware, confirms and proves
the legend. The Frisian names of persons are to be distinguished
by their final 'a', as in Popta, Heemstra, while the names of places
so often end, reflectively, in 'um', at Dokkum, Marsum, Makkum,
Workum, Kollum, Hallum, that it becomes confusing to the
foreigner. The Frisian pet names Baukje, Saskia, are not less
amusing.

* The fisherfolk of Leith are said to be of Jutish origin, and their wives,
who were seen in their distinctive striped dresses hawking fish in the streets
of Edinburgh were, decidedly, of Jutish or Frisian appearance. It would be
interesting to know more of the origin of the fishing village of Cullercoats,
upon the Northumbrian coast, where till recently the women had a
traditional costume of their own; blue serge jacket, short petticoat, wide
skirt, and black straw bonnet. Can they, too, have come from the Frisian
Islands, or from Jutland? In the course of preparing this present book for
illustration some curious early nineteenth-century costume drawings of
the fishwives of Föhr, one of the North Frisian Islands, formerly Danish,
lying off Schleswig, came to light. These had undeniable resemblances to
the costumes of the Dutch Frisians and are suggestive of a peasant culture
ranging from Jutland to the Zuyder Zee. Horace Marryat (brother of the
more famous 'Captain') in his enchanting *Residence in Jutland*, London,
1860, describes the isle of Amak (Amager), opposite Copenhagen,
colonized in 1516 with a colony of Frisians. 'On Shrove Tuesday, up to the
days of Christian v (1670–1799), the Court held a carnival in the island
of Amak, disguising themselves in the habits of North Holland boors,
with great trunk hose, short jackets, and large blue capes; the ladies in
blue petticoats and odd headdresses.' The same author, writing of Fanö,
most northerly of the North Frisian Islands, off the harbour of Esbjerg,
tells us of 'the voluminous petticoats and black masks similar to those worn
at a *bal masqué*, minus the *bavolet*, worn by the women working in the
fields'. They were to keep off the flying sand; but they became the fashion,
and one of the Frisian masks or gags was worn by Queen Dorothea, who
was painted, wearing it, previous to the year 1500.

Leeuwarden itself is charming and pretty as a provincial capital, not less so because of the good looks, the blue eyes, and ash-
blond hair of a great part of the population, those, particularly,
who have come in from the country districts. The Frisians do really
have the appearance of a race apart. A look at the map will show
that another province, Groningen, divides them from the Germans. It is possible that the inhabitants of the old German Grand
Duchy of Oldenbourg, which lies next to Groningen, may resemble
them. But their origin is supposed to have been Slav, not German.
They, more probably, resembled the Wendish population of the
Spreewald, the marshy district near Berlin, and that is very far
removed indeed from Friesland. But, to ourselves, having con-
firmed that the Frisians are a race apart, something added to Holland, but not Dutch by birth, the interest of Frisia is that more
than any other district or province of Europe it approximated to
what we would call a paradise of the farmers and rich peasants.
As in some old legend, the wealthy peasants lived like princes.
Their farmhouses contained great inlaid presses, mirrors in gilded
frames, 'Japanese' porcelain, and silver vessels standing upon
shelves. The presses, in question, were filled with linen and silk
gowns, cups, plates, and coffee-pots of silver, forks, spoons, and
tobacco boxes made of gold, and the jewellers and goldsmiths of
Leeuwarden were famous for two centuries.* These peasants lived
economically for the greater part of the year, but on great holidays, or for a marriage, or the *Kermis,* they installed themselves
in the best inns, took the best boxes at the opera, and 'cracked
in the intervals many a choice bottle of champagne'. And our
informant of these lively doings peeped into a room where
the wife and daughter of a peasant were sitting at work, one
on each side of a table, the mother wearing a casque of gold,
and her daughter one of silver. It is Edmondo de Amicis speaking,
a voluble Italian, who saw it some time in the 1870s. He gives

* Tjeerdt van der Lely was the most celebrated silversmith of Leeuwarden. He made most of the silver objects in the treasure of Dr Popta,
now housed in the Frisian museum. Was he related to Sir Peter Lely,
born van der Faes, at Soest in Westphalia; but his father had changed his
name from van der Faes to Lely?

a quick and brilliant description of the Frisian capital and the best account known to us of the golden helmets of the Frisian women.

De Amicis had come to Leeuwarden on a rainy day and seen no women 'beyond a skinny old hag looking out of window at the weather'. But he was agog to see others, not only for their beauty but because of the gold helmets he had heard of. The evening before, on his arrival, he had caught one glimpse, at a corner, of a group of women's heads strangely shining and glittering, but it was for a moment only, and in the dark. How to see all the fair sex of the capital of Friesland, in full daylight, and for as long as he pleased? It looked like raining all day, and the women would stay indoors. He thought of a clever stratagem. It was the King of Holland's birthday, and he saw a bandsman of the Civic Guard, in plumed hat, walking past, with his trombone under his arm. He followed the musician to the great square; the battalion was formed, the band burst into music, the column moved out of the square, and de Amicis, or so he says, walked with them at the drum major's side.

Instantly, every window opened. Women appeared at them, with the glittering helmets on their heads. Some with silver, some with golden helmets. The battalion turned into one of the principal streets. Leeuwarden, says de Amicis, 'seemed a great barrack full of beardless Cuirassiers'. He continues: 'The shining helmets threw gold and silver reflections on the window panes, and on the varnished doors, and darted lightning rays through the muslin curtains and the flowers in the windows. As we passed I could see reflected in the casques of the girls upon the side walks, the trees, the shop windows, the sky, the Civic Guard, and even my own figure with its dark and ugly attire. At every step I saw something odd. A boy, to tease a little girl, breathes upon her helmet, and the latter angrily scolds at him, and repolishes it with her sleeve, like a soldier whose accoutrements have been dirtied by a companion just before the review. A young man at a window touches with the end of a stick the casque of a young lady at the next window, making it resound, and people turn to look, while the lady blushes and retires. Within the doorway a servant girl arranges her own casque, using that of a friend, who bends prettily before her, as a looking glass. In the vestibule of a house that must be a school, about 50 little girls, all in casques, range themselves silently, two and two, like a regiment of small warriors making ready for a sortie.' De Amicis now enters a private house, armed with a letter of introduction, and demands to see closely the maid Sophia's golden helmet. He compares her pale neck to the white lace of her veil, but Sophia 'remained grave and silent as a statue', and, the examination concluded, 'went out of the room with the slow, majestic step of a tragedy queen'. On the evening of this great day de Amicis amused himself by standing at the door of his hotel, looking at the women and girls with their glittering helmets, 'like a general inspector at the annual review when the soldiers pass before him, one by one, with arms and baggage'. And we have to part from him, but for a few brief moments more, as he prepares himself to leave Leeuwarden for Groningen next morning, 'embittered', characteristically, 'by a regret which I still cherish – that of not having seen the handsome, courageous, and severe daughters of the North skating and sliding on the ice, when they pass, according to Alphonso Esquiroz, wrapped in mists, and crowned with a nimbus of gold and lace, like the fantastic figures in a dream'.

So we turn to Alphonso Esquiroz, and to Henri Havard, for more information. We find this, in Esquiroz, that he was shown a sledge, bearing the date 1793, which was a perfect work of art, the body covered with paintings representing Moses saved from the Nile, while the lower part displayed the star-studded firmament. 'In this little shell, painted red, gilded, and carved in a Chinese style, a young woman sat, and steered herself by means of two iron-shod sticks, flying over the frozen waters with the ability of a swan traversing the air.' We shall see sledges and many objects just as pretty as this in the Frisian museum. What has Henri Havard to say? He describes the three kinds of sledges: the *ijssleede* or little hand sleigh; the *steek-sleedje,* of the sort we have just seen; and the larger carved and gilt sledges drawn by ponies.

He tells us that the Frisian skates were different from the Dutch; formed of a straight iron blade, whereas those of the Dutch had a curving blade. But Havard had heard of skating competitions, when a number of young girls congregated together, and in order to leave their movements quite free from the weight of the woollen stuffs they wear, they strip themselves from their petticoats, not even donning the less graceful but more useful garb of the men. The girls are led to the point of departure, where they unfasten their dresses, unhook their bodices, and at a given signal drop their garments, bound forward, and fly through the air like a shaft from a bow. Where was de Amicis? We mourn his absence as a friend.

But the golden casques or *oorijzers* of the Frisian women, alas, have nearly disappeared. Some persons, romantically minded, would derive them from the 'fact' that the women of the North, especially those of noble birth, wore golden coronets upon their heads. In reality, they are the enlargement of a small cap of gold or silver, set with pear-shaped eardrops, into a golden skullcap, and the whole development of this extraordinary headdress is to be studied in a showcase in the Frisian museum. Upon our first day in Leeuwarden we saw no sign of them at all. Then, from the balcony of my hotel bedroom upon a Sunday morning, I saw an old woman passing in a golden casque. Not more than four or five of the golden helmets did we see, altogether, in Leeuwarden, and all worn by old women : but the old ladies in the Popta alms-house, a few miles from the town, all wore the casques, and upon Sundays you may see a bonnet of jet and feathers worn upright upon the golden helmet. Within a very few years they will be gone entirely, being worn by no one under 70 years of age. We missed, therefore, any opportunity of seeing a golden helmet upon a young girl's head, and have to imagine for ourselves how pretty it must have been, though, of course, it completely hid their ash-blonde hair. Yet it can have been nothing else, in idea, but an image or accentuation of their pale gold locks. What can have been the effect of a town full of women and young girls in golden casques? Looking at those, even upon an old head, we would reply that it is all but impossible to believe the truth, which is that they are an invention of the late eighteenth century, and we are left with an impression of having seen the women of the Ostrogoths, or Visigoths, or some race of blue-blooded barbarians with ash-blonde hair.

But this dress of the Frisian women was not only worn by peasants. It was worn by the Friesland noble ladies, and as late as 1895 could be seen at the opera at The Hague upon a gala night. In this respect it can or could have been compared to the Andalusian dress worn by all classes in Seville. The gala dress of Friesland, as depicted in *The National Costumes of Holland,* comprised the golden helmet or *oorijzer* with a *flodder muts* or soft cap of lace worn over it, and skirts of blue and red flowered taffetas or green and yellow chintz; also they carried purses of embossed black velvet, with silver chains and clasps. But the dresses are more elaborate than that, for the pattern of the taffetas is only on the sleeves and bodice and the basque or short coatee, the skirt being of the plain taffetas or chintz without the flowers. They are, in fact, wide skirts with flowered panels, and both young girls wear over their dresses shawls and aprons, respectively, of black lace upon the blue, and red and white lace upon the green and yellow, so that their costumes are netted or mantilla'd, which, with their black velvet purses, gives to them some curious air of Spain. They wear the coral necklaces of Dutch peasant women, and their golden helmets, which we are more sure than before must be in image or anagram of their pale gold hair, are worn over under-caps, while the flounces of the *flodder muts* – how appropriate a name – fall in pleats upon their necks and hide their ears. In effect, therefore, those are golden casques with immature wings or plumes at the sides, and we are not able to resist thinking how it would have inflamed the Spaniards of 100 or 200 years ago to behold young Frisian ladies of this fatal fairness walking in, say, the whitewashed alleys of Seville under the shadow of the Giralda, or into the cloister of the cathedral planted with orange trees, the Patio de los Naranjos. Under the blue skies of Seville the fair-haired Frisians with their mantillas and their golden caps would be like ghosts from the Visigothic age of Spain, apparitions of the legendary pastures and the lands of milk and cream.

But we now light upon costumes that are yet more entrancing. These were worn in remote districts of Friesland and among other villages at Molkwerum, a little place with never more than 300 or 400 inhabitants called in old books, mysteriously, the 'labyrinth' of Friesland. Molkwerum is but a few miles from Hindeloopen and the costume and language were the same as that of Hindeloopen, but we describe this costume in its present context because it is an instance of that phenomenon we mentioned of country fashions flowering at the very moment of their adoption. It is not, therefore, the old costume of Molkwerum or Hindeloopen. That had died out before this was invented. But this enchantment, of which a pair of specimens are figured in *The National Costumes of Holland,* is derived, in the words of that text, 'from the style favoured by the ladies of the upper classes towards 1810, when it was worn with the high-waisted Empire dress, and showed the influence of the masculine "topper" '. They are peasant girls in top hats. But what top hats! Their dresses, though, are eighteenth century. And we must delay in order to describe the fascination of this bucolic poetry. In the first place, both girls wear milkmaids' aprons, one a blue apron with a yoke of blue and white checked cotton, the other, a terracotta linen apron with a yoke of yellow and self-coloured chequers. The first girl has a purplish, plum-coloured skirt under her blue apron, and her bodice is of mauve cotton with conventional flowers upon it in red, blue, white, and yellow. Her shawl, like that of a fishergirl, is of red and white checked Indian cotton. The other, who has a dark blue skirt below her terracotta apron, wears a scarlet bodice with a Turkish pattern of flowers and leaves in blue, green, black, and yellow. It is like a design on Turkish tiles, or on the silks of Brusa, but it has shoulder straps which are reminiscent of Swedish peasant dress, like the apron dresses of the Dalecarlians by the lakes and birch woods in the pale North. She has no shawl to go with this, but she wears a collar or fichu of blue, darker blue, and white cotton, and her sleeves are red and white in stripes of varying widths.

And their 'toppers'?* The wonder is that both are wearing the golden casques under their top hats, but all we can see are the golden rosettes which are the terminals, and the golden pins at the corners of their foreheads or on their temples. The gold helmets, or *oorijzers,* are altogether hidden. The 'topper' of the girl in the purplish skirt with the red and white checked cotton shawl is a tall hat of hatters' plush, with a narrow brim, trimmed at the top with gold galloon and a green silk fringe, a discovery which puts to shame the sealing wax on the top hats of members of 'Pop', worn with mere buttonholes and coloured waistcoats at Eton on the 'Fourth of June'. Moreover, the 'topper' of this Frisian peasant girl has a green silk ribbon tied in a bow round the crown. Her companion who, for another touch of enchantment, is carrying a basket of strawberries in one hand, wears a straw 'topper' of large proportions with a trimming of green ribbons at the top, but covering a wider field, and brown ribbons round the crown. Both girls, as we have said, show the golden pins and rosettes at their temples and have, also, the fascinating folds or pleats of their lace or net caps falling in front of their ears and upon their shoulders. They are fruit sellers, vendors of strawberries, but in what Elysian village street? Upon what lawns? To what music of a hidden orchestra? It is difficult, indeed almost impossible, to credit this beautiful feat of invention to a village inhabited, when Havard went there, by 220 Calvinists, 70 Mennonites, 11 Catholics, and two Lutherans. Of the Mennonites more later : but we depart reluctantly from Molkwerum, looking back once more at this pair of Frisian maidens in their top hats, standing arm-in-arm together, and trying to imagine for ourselves a village architecture and a male species worthy of them.

* Compare, for another late instance of country fashions, and one of the most beautiful local costumes in the whole of Spain, the top hat and white ostrich plumes worn by the women of Pueblo de Guzman, near Huelva, in Estremadura. This can be nothing else than an echo of the riding fashion for Parisian ladies of the First Empire, though how this had permeated to a remote village in the south of Spain it is impossible to tell. Perhaps it had been brought back by some nurse or servant girl. The ruched black skirts and flowered bonnets of Montehermoso, in the same province, are no less curious.

However, the most extraordinary creation of all is still to be described. This, too, is entirely local in the sense of being confined to a certain district and rarely to be seen in the streets of Leeuwarden, the capital. Mijnheer van Buijtenen, who wrote the book on Hindeloopen, told me that Stavoren was its centre, but it is figured in *The National Costume of Holland* as coming from Makkum about 10 miles away. Makkum, we should add, is a little village on the Zuyder Zee, famed for its blue and white china, which makes its inhabitants not less curious when we consider how far distant they were from the celestial kilns and pagodas. It was, too, a centre of the East Indian trade, with the result that Oriental materials were imported for its costumes. But the dress that we are describing was worn, not by peasant women, but by ladies of the neighbourhood and the wives of rich merchants. It consists of a short, open, blue silk coat, surely of Chinese influence, and a skirt which, we are told, is of Oriental design adapted by Occidental manufacturers. However this may be, it is unsurpassed in decorative boldness, a chintz skirt of a white ground printed with a broad repeating pattern of figures of men in long wigs and coats standing on little pedestals or platforms, great vases with a huge conventional red flower put in them, red or blue roses with their leaves, garlands and ribbons, and red birds (parrots?) sometimes with blue wings, a chintz fantasy, in fact, of the utmost poetry and beauty, the convention of design being somewhat similar to that of the figures upon linen damask tablecloths. Those, when seen in England, and they may have scenes of hunting boars or bears, or stag-hunts, or even formal garden scenes, are given, loosely, the date and title of Queen Anne and are said to be of Flemish origin, but the design upon the chintz skirt makes me wonder if they did not come from Friesland. This beautiful skirt and blue silk coat are worn with black silk mittens, but it is the Mikkum lady's hat which is inimitable and nowhere to be equalled.

It is what was called a *Deutsche muts* or German cap. Similar hats are said to have been worn in parts of Germany, perhaps in the Grand Duchy of Oldenbourg, as long ago as 1736. We would describe it as a cartwheel hat, flat and round like a tambour, but with the head at one circumference so that it projects forward, the entire brim having a deep fringe hanging down. First of all the hair was drawn back and coiled round a pad of cotton wool, under a cap of black sateen. Over this, the *oorijzer*, the golden casque of the Frisians, was worn, and the ornamental ends of that hung down below the ears. The foundation of the *Deutsche muts* was a white lace *coiffe* of especially fine texture which was stretched tightly over the gigantic wire brim of the cartwheel or tambour, so that it fell like a fringe all round the brim. The Frisian ladies in their cartwheel hats had a walk and a carriage conditioned by their fantastic headgear. But there were various forms of the *Deutsche muts.* For outdoors a huge yellow straw hat was worn with the lace brim, but lined with pink and blue chintz and there were immense red and gold ribbons attached to it, ribbons which came down to the waist and were like the coloured streamers of a bird of paradise.

Edmondo de Amicis, missing from the ice carnival, now returns to us, for he states that the custodian of the museum at Leeuwarden in his time had seen a hat of this pattern upon the head of an old lady, some years before, when there was a festival for the arrival of the King of Holland. There were persons still living, therefore, in 1860 who in their youth had worn the *Deutsche muts.* De Amicis describes the hat as having the dimensions of an ordinary coffee table, with a straw superstructure with a brim of the same size 'wanting on one side so that it has a semi-circular form. The circular piece of wood', he continues, 'is ornamented with a deep fringe, and has a small opening in which the head is inserted. When this is done, the straw hat, which is separate, is put on and stretched over it like an awning over a booth and the edifice is complete. When the wearer,' he concludes, 'entered a church, she unroofed herself, so to speak, in order not to take up too much space, and put it on again on coming out, an operation which was thought very convenient and the hat itself extremely elegant.' Certainly I would describe the *Deutsche muts* as the most extreme invention ever made in hats. They form an extraordinary pair, the

12 *Langs de Vecht*

13 *A summer afternoon on the Schermerhorn*

two persons figured in *The National Costumes of Holland,* he in his thick brown overcoat, buttoned all down the front, black beaver hat with shallow crown and holding in his hand a long clay pipe, of old the ensign of a Dutchman. Its place till lately was taken by the East Indian cigar, but Havard, entering the Burgomaster's room in the Town Hall at Leeuwarden, was amused by the table covered with green baize and the long ready-filled clay pipe from Gouda, placed before each chair. The pale blue silk coat, embroidered muslin fichu and chintz skirt with figures, flowers, and birds, worn by the lady in the *Deutsche muts,* are impossible to forget. It is the lining of her immense hat with glazed pink and blue chintz which is especially remarkable, and we shall find other instances of this lining of straw hats with coloured chintzes, and come to the opinion that it is a beautiful discovery in dress. Her red and gold streamers are the climax to this most peculiar of costumes. Odd as it may be, it is not more curious than other specimens of the *Deutsche muts* to be seen in the collection of dresses in the Frisian Museum. There is one that is more a parachute than a cartwheel hat, and another which is a yellow straw, lined with pleated lace or muslin and a work of art in itself, beside the shade and beauty conferred upon its gold-casqued wearer.

What can have been the appearance of the single street of Makkum with its old houses, when the patrician ladies of the *Deutsche muts,* probably not more than six or eight all told in so small a place, were abroad in their great hats? Upon a weekday, we would have it, not a Sunday when the blue and white china kilns would be closed, but for some celebration, or a wedding? Their hats and dresses have something, it is undeniable, of the German sixteenth century, but as though Altdorfer, or more still, one of the German–Swiss primitives, Urs Graf or Niklaus Manuel Deutsch, had been awoken from his sleep, been shown prints and drawings of the Far Indies and told to design hats and dresses for a party of ladies returned from China in the reign of our Queen Anne, who yet insisted upon wearing under their hats the latest invention, which was the golden casque or skull cap. But it is a fact that the domestic setting for these noble or burgher ladies of the *Deutsche muts* was not less strange and beautiful.

In the Frisian Museum at Leeuwarden, beside the Hindeloopen rooms that we shall mention later, there is an interior from Workum, another village or small town upon the Zuyder Zee, less than 10 miles from Makkum. This is one of the most graceful and delightful 'coloured' rooms that I have ever seen. I call it 'coloured' because the walls are not done in fresco. It is not one of the painted rooms of Holland, of which we shall visit shortly a supreme example. It is merely a panelled room with cupboards of blue and white china and tile pictures from the kilns of Makkum. This interior is of entirely different character from the Hindeloopen rooms, belonging, as it were, to another country of the imagination. Walls and cupboards painted in an apple-blossom pink, for I can think of no other name for it, it is fresher and gayer in effect than *bois de rose*. The date of this room is given as 1797, but we are concerned with a remote country district at the end of the world when the bucolic arts were at their zenith and time and fashion were in a vacuum. Anywhere else, therefore, it would be a room of 1770. The blue and white of the Makkum ware, together with the apple-blossom walls and cupboards, make an interior that is unsurpassed in gaiety and high spirits. It must have been a happy world that could find such felicities lying ready to its fingertips. But there is a painted table in the room of even more distant provenance, for it comes from Ameland, one of the Frisian islands which was famous for its long-tailed black Frisian mares, and we must believe, on such evidence, that there, too, in that remote island there was a flowering of the arts of decoration.

In Leeuwarden itself, for we cannot linger for ever in the Frisian Museum, but leave it, to return later, our steps are directed to the Stadhuis, where we miss the long clay pipes of Henri Havard, but are rewarded by the stucco walls and restored panelling of the courtroom in which a wedding is in progress. In the anteroom on either wall there are late eighteenth-century paintings, head and shoulders only, of young women wearing the golden head irons, as some writers like to call them, but we prefer the Frisian golden casque or helmet. And there is another charming building, the Princessehof, the palace of Marie-Louise of Hesse-Cassel, mother of the last Frisian Stadhouder, known comically and endearingly as *Marijke Meu,* 'Aunt Mary', and built for her by her architect Coulon. It is now a museum of Chinese and Indonesian works of art, but has fine stucco ceilings and one room with painted leather wall decorations on a golden ground. For the experience that followed and brought me to the most beautiful room that I saw in Holland, I am indebted to Mijnheer van Buijtenen, a young man attached as librarian to the State Archives, who introduced himself at the Stadhuis, accompanied us to the Princessehof and struck a pleasant note of an old and vanished world by proposing to speak Latin to me, but I preferred Italian. It was on his suggestion that we went down the little lane at the side of the Princessehof to an unpretentious, indeed a very small red brick building, for it is referred to in no guide book or other literature that I have seen.

This is the house of Antoine Coulon, the architect, and I do not know whether he was a Frenchman or a Fleming, but probably in Friesland, the paradise of religious minorities, he was a Huguenot. Coulon appears also to have been a printer.* There is an entrance hall of rather coarse and heavy stucco, not work of the first order, and then the doors are opened into the rooms, or rather into a small anteroom and a saloon and dining-room, that must have looked out upon a little formal garden at the back. These rooms are always kept shuttered and in darkness, for the house is unused except as an overflow for the State Archives. The electric light will be turned on in the little anteroom while someone goes into the next room in darkness and opens up the shutters. What is then revealed is one of the richest schemes of decoration ever seen and nothing less than a small masterpiece of the applied arts.

The walls are hung with painted canvas of a blue-green ground, the colour, could we so describe it, of the outside of an avocado

---

* Antoine Coulon was son of a French *charpentier* and *menuisier* and was born in Amsterdam.

pear, upon which is painted an all-over design of abstract fruits and flowers, pomegranate, fig, or pineapple motifs, for it is only possible to give approximate names to what is purely of the imagination. The effect, owing to the disposition of the pattern, is that they are trellised or espaliered until, looking closer, we see that they are trees or columns repeating every four times and hung from head to foot with the fruits and flowers of an imaginary East Indies. This sensational scheme of decoration is bold and fanciful beyond experience. It is in the richest, late Louis xiv manner of 1690–1715, though executed, as I imagine, a generation later in distant Friesland, and intended, no doubt, to be Chinese or Indian as that term was understood.* Upon the morning we first saw it there was brilliant sunlight in the room, it was a July day, but on another occasion we went there at night and the effect was not less superb, though for full richness it needs, of course, the flickering candlelight. I should like to see it, too, upon a bright winter morning with deep snow outside. The farther room has beautiful wall decorations in a similar but slighter manner, more like a painted Chinese wallpaper and intended to give contrast. I would say that these rooms in the Coulon Huis at Leeuwarden, not for richness of material and money spent, but for bewildering intoxication of effect, are to be compared to the circular mirror-room of Cuvilliès in silver and blue and to the bedroom and hunting-room in silver upon a yellow ground at the pavilion of the Amalienburg. Those are Rococo at its moment of greatest delicacy, these are Baroque; but the one cost a fortune and the other was executed at no more cost than prepared canvas and a few pots of paint .Upon entering this farther room for the first time my enjoyment and sense of discovery were made complete when I found two portraits upon the walls of Frisian noble ladies wearing the immense *Deutsche muts* or cartwheel hat. It was then and there

---

* We are informed by Dr Ozinga that these painted canvases were removed to Leeuwarden a few years ago from an old house, Oude Ebbingestraat, in Groningen. This house, of about 1760, was destroyed by the Germans; but the painted canvases are characteristic of Groningen, where all eighteenth-century decoration and furniture were very Baroque in style.

that I was told these hats came from Stavoren and were worn only in that neighbourhood, but whether this pair of portraits were part of the original decoration of the Coulon House I was not able to find out. At least, with their cartwheel brims, their coloured ribbons and hidden golden helmets, they give the last touch of fantasy to this thing of beauty.

But it is time to leave Leeuwarden for the day and go into the country. Our first choice was Dokkum, having read somewhere that the Stadhuis contained 'two rooms that are the most curious specimens that can be seen of the architecture of Louis xv applied to municipal purposes'. Besides, Dokkum is 25 miles north of Leeuwarden towards the Frisian islands and in a direction where, normally, one would never go. This is an opportunity of seeing the pastures of the Frisians, the great farmsteads standing apart, dwelling house and farm buildings all under one roof which is part tile, part thatch, and with every appearance of being self-contained. These farms can be seen lying out in every direction, a quarter or half a mile apart, with their black and white herds of Frisian cows which are their fortune. Within a few miles, so completely have we entered into this bucolic paradise of the farmer and rich peasant that it is bewildering to think of these separate farmsteads in their hundreds and easy to believe that this was the place for fugitives to hide in during the German occupation : few villages, but farms in hundreds and in thousands – not so much water as in North Holland, but only occasional long, straight canals leading for miles, and not the little water alleys. The accent in Friesland is not upon the village but the farm. We are making towards Ameland whence came the best black Frisian horses, used in England, paradoxically, to draw our funeral hearses, but there is no sign more of the *boerenchais,* the high tilburys or dog carts seen by Havard of which he says : 'The model is that of a century old, the box is handsomely sculptured, highly coloured and gilt, and the black horses are ornamented with red bows.' These vehicles were always driven at a fast trot; nor did we see a Frisian trotting match for which they were nearly as famous as for their skating contests. The Frisian Museum has a whole showcase full of whips which were given as prizes at the trotting matches, one of them, unexpectedly, having been put up in honour of the birthday of the King of Rome. But the wealth of these pastures was their cheese and butter, and this paradise of the farmers achieved its greatest prosperity towards the middle of the nineteenth century, when London was their foreign market. The butter was packed in little barrels made of Russian oak, which were brought from the farms to the *Waag* or weigh house of the different country towns, where it was sampled, weighed, and had stamped upon it the city arms; after which it was taken to Harlingen and put aboard a steamer bound for London.

Dokkum had a famous flax market, where the flax merchants of England, France, and Germany had their agents. But also it was celebrated for its Friesland butter. It must have been extremely prosperous all through the eighteenth century until the Napoleonic wars. It is at the end of everything, with the sea a few miles away, and only the isles of Ameland and Terschelling beyond it, not a town, therefore, to which it might be thought that the refinements of one of the great movements in art had penetrated. Upon the way there it seemed unlikely that the interior of the Stadhuis could be worth a visit. Dokkum is a small town with a few old houses. The Stadhuis, a delightful red brick building of a particularly sharp or bright red brick, is reminiscent partly of an Arcadian harbour building and in part of the red brick houses in Randolph Caldecott's drawings for *John Gilpin*. It stands on the canal bank and has a high, white wooden cupola or belfry, which gives it character. One of the two promised rooms of the interior is disappointing, but the other deserves a considerably longer journey than that from Leeuwarden to Dokkum. It is the *Raadzaal* or Court Room and is, in fact, one of the sights of Friesland, being as good a painted room of the early eighteenth century as is to be seen anywhere in Europe, G. B. Tiepolo excepted. Italian painted rooms of the *settecento* suffer, invariably, from inferior workmanship in their surroundings, the stucco and woodwork being of poor quality compared with the paintings, perhaps for the reason that the best Venetian workmen went to London or to Dublin.

But the *Raadzaal* at Dokkum has a glorious Rococo ceiling, much resembling good stucco work in Dublin houses; the panelling in reddish wood, though repainted in questionable taste, is of superb quality, and the array of high-backed chairs for the burgomaster and town councillors, doubtless by the same hand that carved the panelling, would fetch a small fortune in the London sale-room. Compared with this room at Dokkum the painted room in the Stadhuis at Edam is merely quaint and bucolic. For the paintings, four or five big panels upon the long wall, are as good in decoration as the best Gobelin tapestries, mythological scenes with backgrounds of architecture, signed and dated 'D. Reynes, 1763', the work of a painter who is quite unknown to fame. They are first rate in colour, the sort of decorative paintings one expects to find, and looks for in vain, in monasteries in Austria, with Italy near by and under Venetian influence, and which it almost passes belief to discover in this remote place of 4,000 inhabitants in distant Friesland. But good as is his colour, the talent of D. Reynes showed itself to more advantage still in his panels in grisaille or different shades of sepia; in the panels of the overdoors, which are little triumphs of skilful and graceful management, and above all in the big sepia painting over the mantelpiece, which is a decorative masterpiece in little, and considering its limitations could not be more personal in style. The subjects of the overdoors are groups of cupids; but how much better these are in style and handling than similar panels by Jacob de Wit, who only attempted to make his paintings into imitations of stone bas reliefs. This overmantel grisaille painting has for subject a seated figure of Minerva (?); but as a decorative composition and with its Rococo frame it is worthy of the Villa Valmarana, and brings a breath of blue sky and trellised vineyard to this north shore of the Zuyder Zee. In this manner have the Latins triumphed 17 centuries later over the barbarian Frisians; but then we remember this red brick building on a Dutch canal, the Burgomaster in full-bottomed wig, with long clay pipe, and his tobacco-smoking councillors, and in the knowledge that this is one of the most graceful and beautiful of eighteenth-century interiors we wonder what other surprises the little towns of Friesland may have to yield.

Half-way from Dokkum to Harlingen, near the sandy coast, there is the village of Sint Anna Parochie where Rembrandt was married in 1634 to Saskia van Ulenborgh, whose blue eyes and Frisian ash-blonde hair are immortalized in his paintings. She was the daughter of a Friesland lawyer and brought him a large dowry. He was 28 years old, extravagant, and full of hopes. Ten years later Saskia died, ruin and bankruptcy followed, and Rembrandt was to become the familiar and prematurely aged subject of his self-portraits. Harlingen, a few miles farther on, is the chief port in Friesland. 'It was at Harlingen', to quote the eloquent sentence in Henri Havard, 'that the London meat, poultry, and vegetable merchants arrive to carry off the Friesland cattle and the crops, thus putting, according to the French proverb, "butter in their spinach" and offering to the blonde misses of those great writers, Thackeray and Dickens, the butter for their interminable "tartines"!' And he tells us that on 'its canals the bullocks are embarked with sheep, pigs, and poultry which go to help fatten our neighbours on the other side of the Channel. Through its basins on their way to the sea pass mountains of cheese, fruit, eggs, which go to be swallowed up in England.' But we believe that this statement raises, and at the same time solves, a very minor problem in aesthetics. It concerns the rare breed of fowls, the bearded Polands to be seen in Hondecoeter's paintings, and also the Dutch 'everyday layers', *chitteprats*, or silver and gold pencilled Hamburghs. The origin of the latter has always been a mystery, for the one thing certain is that they did not come from Hamburg. It is our belief that crates of these curious but beautiful-looking fowls could have been seen at Harlingen in the act of their being embarked for England, and that their origin was in Friesland. The bearded, crested Poland poultry that, hen or rooster, have the proud bearing of Rembrandt's *Polish Rider* and the plumes and spangles of a Zulu chief leading his Impi, or merely pulling a rickshaw in the streets of Durban, are to be assigned to Friesland, together with the silver pencilled Hamburgh, most delicate in marking of all domestic fowls. It is an enchantment to think that they may have strutted in the street of

Makkum upon that week-day morning, near to the kilns of blue
and white, at that moment when the door of the patrician house
opened and the young lady came forth in her coloured chintz skirt
and huge cartwheel hat.

Franeker, a little town five miles away which had once a university, is so small a place that we can pass through it in a few
moments, or spend the rest of our lives in its vacuum. We chose
the former course, or would still be in Franeker, walking into the
church late in the autumn afternoons to contemplate the great
tomb slabs of the learned professors set upright against the walls
of red sandstone, or great monoliths of darker granite, works
of the *antyksnyders* or Frisian sculptors, and wondering whether
among these dead there is not an alchemist or two, or disciple
of Doctor Faustus. Old gabled houses are in quantity, but the
appropriate ornament of this dormant town is perhaps the planetarium constructed in the back parlour of his own dwelling, which
is one of the old houses, by a wool-comber of Franeker called Eise
Eisinga, a name that for all its Frisian terminations could appear
among the lesser executives whose names are flashed for a long
moment of tedium upon the cinema screen. The planetarium was
made late in the eighteenth century and is wound up by clock-
work once a week. We did not see it. We missed the little room
with walls painted the blue of the skies, now much faded. We
never saw the rotating ceiling for the vault of the heavens, nor the
gilded balls that revolve on their courses round the sun and represent the planets. Its mysteries are shown by the light of a solitary
candle, and we could have asked whether the present custodian,
like 'the very tired young woman' of Mr E. V. Lucas in 1904, or
the 'half-servant, half-bourgeoise, who as she pointed to each
object explained its meaning in a monotonous voice as if repeating a lesson', of Henri Havard, a generation before that, is the
descendant of Eise Eisinga. Some movements of the planetarium
are accomplished only once in 30 years. Such things are possible
in the little town of Franeker, which we would point to as a likely
hiding place for Doctor Faustus. But, too hurried, we missed the
planetarium; as, also, the Stadhuis, where we would have seen

embroideries by Anna Maria van Schuurman and the portrait of this learned, gifted, and saintly woman hanging among those of the old professors. But of Anna Maria van Schuurman, more presently.

I had looked forward to Bolsward as being the most interesting and beautiful of the small towns of Friesland, and was disappointed. Certainly, it has old houses, one in particular with a lovely Rococo fanlight opposite the Stadhuis, but it is this building itself, described parrot-like by all writers and travellers as having the finest Renaissance façade in all Holland, which is the big deception. The Stadhuis is a brick and stone building of the same character as the Meat Market of Lieven de Key at Haarlem, that is to say, it is in the style that we should call in England James I, or early Jacobean. The stone stair in front is much later and was added in the middle of the eighteenth century, but the far famed stone satyr lamps upon the balustrade fall short of the descriptions and are as nothing compared to the masks and balcony carvings of Catania or Noto. This is Holland; and we miss the golden stone and sunny skies of Sicily. Dutchmen, who sailed so far upon distant oceans, must have been aware of this, for their old word for an orange is a Messina-apple. The Stadhuis of Bolsward, however, has an octagonal steeple of lead and timber in its upper storeys, and it is of this that Mr E. V. Lucas remarks that it is an Oriental bell tower and that 'this constant recurrence of Oriental freakishness in the architecture of Dutch towns is an effect to which one never quite grows accustomed'. He must have intended by this that the steeple with its diminishing storeys was like a Chinese pagoda, but, in fact, it does not resemble a pagoda at all. Like similar towers in Amsterdam and all over Holland, it is the early prototype in lead and timber of the stone spires of our London city churches. The Stadhuis, we have to admit, has been effectively and hideously restored, and there is nothing else much to admire in Bolsward.

But a few miles away the lakes and meres begin. Upon a summer day hundreds of white sails are to be seen over the low meadows, all collected in certain directions, and so numerous that they are like the swarms or clouds of white 'cabbage' butterflies that are described in letters to the newspapers. They are the Friesland regattas or, more probably, and we will leave it so, this is 'Sneek Week', Sneek being pronounced in Dutch in the same way that we say the word 'snake', and a local festival of which the praise and renown were sung to us upon many mouths. Sneek, delightful name, is a town that we are approaching at 50 or 60 miles an hour along a level road, and Sneek Week is the regatta held every year in August upon the Sneeker Meer. From all indications it must be very gay; while, in winter, there is skating upon the frozen lakes. Let us hope that the skating contests are still as stimulating and seductive as those described at second-hand by the warm-blooded and impressionable Latins, Havard, de Amicis, Esquiroz, of two generations ago! At night, we wonder, do they still dance the national dance, the *skotse trije,* in the courtyard of some ancient building, in the golden casques of the old Frisians, or in hiking dress to relayed music by the B.B.C.? We did not dare enquire.

But in Sneek, a little town with a wholly delightful air of happiness and contentment, and with the proportion of good looking young women of typical Frisian appearance outnumbering the less well favoured, there is at least one beautiful building, the Stadhuis. This really is as fanciful as an Apulian or Sicilian building yet, withal, typically, delightfully, and altogether entirely Dutch, and in the opinion of the present writer who knows well the Rococo of Austria and Germany, it could be Dutch only and of no other nationality whatsoever. A high, square, dark brick building with a white-painted wooden belfry and a staircase in front. The richness of effect is in the balustrading and in the stone ornaments upon the brick, figures of cupids flying head downwards, an unusual attitude though logical, for we must impute to the winged children the freedom of their wings. They should soar and hover, and not alight, always, feet foremost, with the stiff flight of the helicopter. Here, in the Town Hall of Sneek, they are a little cramped, it is true, by the shape of the blocks of stone.

The balustrading of the double flight of stone stairs and the lanterns at top and bottom are elegant and fanciful, and with the rich traceries of the overdoor all composes into a satisfying effect of ornament and line. It is almost with trepidation that one enters such a building for fear of disappointment. But, on that late afternoon, the pair of heavy Rococo wooden doors were unlocked and open. We saw the interior of the Stadhuis alone and undisturbed. A good entrance hall with stucco decorations; but I hurried upstairs, fearing locked doors, and found myself in as beautiful an interior of the eighteenth century as I have ever seen, a work of art of which no warning whatsoever had come to us, and I have to conclude that this is its first mention in the English language. It is a *chinoiserie* room painted entirely in shades of green and gold, one of the most complete and perfect examples of this style of decoration, deriving from that great age of civilization, the eighteenth century, the more curious to our own eyes because we had been assured only a few days before, by an eminent Dutch authority, that no rooms of this description were to be found in Holland, and not less odd and improbable when it is considered that this room in Chinese style was intended for the deliberations of the Burgomaster and his councillors. It is a superb scheme of decoration. Big painted wall panels of *chinoiserie* subjects; a lovely and elegant stucco ceiling; Rococo wall lights; and as at Dokkum a splendid array of armchairs of the period, of green and gold, here, to match the painted decorations. The painted rooms in the Town Halls of Sneek and Dokkum, and in the Coulon House at Leeuwarden, are not only to be numbered among the artistic treasures of Friesland and of Holland, but they are part of the beauties of Europe. Why is it that all writers have neglected them? But even now, the tale of what is to be found in Friesland is incomplete and we have to leave this glimpse of the Burgomaster and his councillors in their heavy wigs, half-obscured in the tobacco smoke from their long clay pipes, against a *chinoiserie* background from the brush of an unknown painter, in favour of another of the 'dead' towns upon the Zuyder Zee, a little seaport in which the inhabitants robed themselves in Oriental costumes and passed their lives in what must have been equivalent to an opium dream of distant lands and exotic fancies, born of the tales told by homecoming sailors.

II

The name of the little town is Hindeloopen, with an import as pretty as it sounds, for it means 'stag-hunt' or 'deer run' and infers that there was a forest, once, along that empty shore. It is, indeed, bleak and deserted, beyond imagining, nothing but a lonely church tower and a few houses huddled together under the dyke wall as though hiding from the sea, a place no bigger than a large village with, it could be, 1,000 inhabitants, no more, and two or three little streets of houses when you come down into it from the road along the sea wall. This is Hindeloopen, famous for its painted wooden furniture and fantastic costume, and it cannot have had a bigger population than it has today. At the time we saw it there was not a single ship lying in its harbour. As it is now the little town can be seen completely in a few moments for it has nothing of interest except the few old dresses in the little museum. The glories of its past, sumptuary glories they were of dress and ornament, have to be pieced together from these, from the accounts of old travellers, and from the two Hindeloopen rooms in the Frisian Museum at Leeuwarden.

One house only retains its original furniture and decorations, and we did not see this. Not a single specimen of the Hindeloopen costume is still worn. None has been worn, in fact, for some 70 or 80 years. All we could see, the museum excepted, was a small antique shop with a pair of painted cupboards, one genuine and the other fake, but the new was as good as the old, and one was left to conjecture who can be these craftsmen who still execute decorations as graceful as any of the Venetian *settecento*. All, or nearly all, the original furniture has left Hindeloopen long ago for private collections, where much of it, indeed, may pass for Venetian painted furniture. This little town had its arts, its special costume, its architecture, and its peculiar language or dialect of Frisian that was only spoken within its walls.

Now the mystery of Hindeloopen is that while these arts flourished they were not recognized. So extraordinary a community and such a flowering of the arts within a small compass cannot have existed since the early Italian Renaissance; we feel almost tempted to write, all differences taken into account, since Hellenic times. Blaeu, the geographer, only says of Hindeloopen that it is a small town, the port of which is hardly known and without any great importance. Guicciardini, and the later author of the *Délices des Pays Bas*, barely condescend to mention it. No one, it is clear, thought anything of Hindeloopen. Its inhabitants were mere mariners and fishermen. They sailed, in the summer, to the ports of Norway, where they loaded timber and brought it to Hoorn, to Enkhuizen, and to Amsterdam. In the Dutch harbours they were paid their profits, and spent them largely in the warehouses of the Dutch East India Company, buying chintzes and Indian stuffs which they took home to their wives. That, and an influence from Norway or from Scandinavia, are said to be the sources of the Hindeloopen arts. For in the winter the mariners remained at home. They passed the time in painting and carving. Such is a plausible explanation, but the truth is not so simple.

Let us hear what Henri Havard, the discoverer of this little place, has to say of Hindeloopen. 'Of the 200 houses,' he writes, 'remaining of the old town, 50 or 60 are built on the same plan, being the same height, having the same frontage and placed side by side in the same spot. This model house,' he continues, '60 times repeated cannot be the result of accident. . . . The decorations of carved and gilded palms and love-knots, relieved by the strangest painting possible to imagine, have no equal except in Persian art. As a rule the colours are loud and gaudy, red or rose, green or blue. . . . Most of the single pieces of furniture, such as tables and stands, stoves and sledges, are ornamented with red and blue palms, around which are interlaced numbers of cupids of dark rose – the whole on a red ground. Sometimes these consistently recurring cupids are placed, always in dark rose, among a bed of blue flowers against a background of red, lightened here and there by white dots and touches of gold. But this *mélange* of discordant colours produces a harmonious and dazzling effect, which I can only liken to the cachemires of India. This same style of ornamentation is adopted in private houses though the colours are somewhat modified. Red yields place to dark blue, and flowers, figures, love-knots, and palms are toned down into soft blue, green, and white, on a background of the finest shade of indigo.' In Havard's time, the 60s or 70s of last century, the Hindeloopen costume had nearly disappeared. It was only worn by two old women, who put it on when a foreigner came to the town, and who were summoned by Havard and rewarded with a florin.

An important point of argument is that the arts of Hindeloopen were not peasant arts. The Hindeloopers were not workers in the fields. It is this that made them different from the communities of peasants or mountaineers, and put them apart from the peasant arts of such places as Mezökövesd in Hungary or the centres of peasant art in Roumania or Slovakia. But neither were they mere fishermen like the population of Volendam or Marken. The Hindeloopers were mariners and sea captains and their families, and we hope to prove that a proportion of them, if only from their religious practices, were possessed of wealth. Lastly, it must be emphasized that they were, entirely, a community apart. Neither their arts nor their costume resembled those of the rest of Friesland. Their women wore neither the golden casque of the Frisians nor the cartwheel *Deutsche muts*; while the interiors of their houses were in another style from those of nearby Stavoren or Workum.

The pair of rooms in the museum at Leeuwarden form the most complete illustration of the arts of Hindeloopen, though objects from the island of Ameland and other places have been added, the waxwork figures, as always, are hideous and disturbing, and the life and soul of the rooms have fled. But it could not be otherwise in the most ideal and Utopian of museums. They spell death, and the living pulse has ceased to beat. The smaller room has blue and white tiles from Makkum to the height of six feet, and white tiles above with a faint blue pattern, while the painted furniture is on a ground of white and yellow. The bed, as at Marken, is contrived like a ship's bunk in the wall, showing that the arts of Hindeloopen are those of the harbour, not the soil. The larger room is more gaily coloured still, though deadened by the wax-work figures, but it is to be remarked that these two rooms of the late seventeenth and early eighteenth centuries contain almost too orthodox a collection of the painted furniture, the choice, it could be, of a museum official with a boring mind. They have become in the process of their installation rooms not of the two centuries named, but of those years in which they were torn from their setting at Hindeloopen and put up in the Frisian Museum. There is nothing to equal in lively grace the painted cupboard that we saw at Hindeloopen, nor the collection of exquisite dresses housed in the little town museum. The person who made this selection of objects seems to have fought shy of the Oriental influence and avoided it, if possible. There are painted wooden drinking vessels much resembling, it cannot be denied, those of the Gudsbrandal and Telemarken districts of Norway. They are unmistakably Scandinavian in influence. But the painted cradles, the sledges and the wooden bed steps show the curious Indian and Persian idiom. The cradles have great painted whorls of leaves with birds perching on the foliage. The bed steps, a peculiar and necessary invention by which the Hindeloopers clothed in who knows what night garments, mounted into their ships' bunks, are particularly beautiful in design and ornament, portable pieces of furniture painted on the sides with great *papegaaien* or parrots in bright green and yellow, their heads and beaks and bird chests bursting forth in relief as part of the shape of these portable steps or ladders.

Drawings of the beautiful Hindeloopen costumes are, unfortunately, few in number. A drawing of 1688 in the museum at Leeuwarden is a view of Dutch boors in baggy breeches, anywhere, and infers that up till then the peculiar features of the dress were in an embryonic state, or in suspense. There is a woman in a high cylindrical fur headdress and most of the men are wearing round fur hats. But that is all. Maaskamp in his *Costumes des Pays Bas*, 1798, a tolerable costume book, has a coloured plate in which the extravagant beauties of the Hindeloopen dresses are

14   *Open lucht*

15 *Traditional costume in Staphorst*

revealed, at last, and we are looking at figures as sumptuous as those to be met in the streets and courts of Isfahan during the reign of Shah Abbas, and as fanciful as the Orientals, Turks, or Mamelukes in Carpaccio's paintings, with this prime difference, that the Hindeloopers are clothed not in silks, but in flowered cottons. The drawing in Maaskamp is of a servant girl pushing her mistress in a painted sledge on the canal, and at first sight they could be Orientals from some frostbound East Indies of the imagination, for both are clothed from head to foot in flowery patterns, their skirts and sleeves are like long dressing gowns, and they wear something resembling a folded turban on their heads. The sleigh, we note, is after the style of the painted furniture of Hindeloopen on that sparkling, frosty morning.

But, for a fuller account there is only one authority to rely upon, the joint authors of *The National Costumes of Holland*. Four plates of this monumental work are devoted to the Hindeloopen costume, and the following information, with all due acknowledgement, is derived from them. Their first illustration is a more detailed adaptation of the plate from Maaskamp. We learn that the peculiar and distinctive headdress of the Hindeloopen women consisted of a circular erection of stiffened linen, covered with red baize and open at the top. Over this, the married woman wore a cap of fine muslin with a *zondoek* or hat scarf of red and white checked Indian cotton. Hence their turbans. But the minutiae of detail in this fantastic, small community! Their corset laces were of red and yellow unless they were in mourning, when the laces were deep blue and green. And the ends of these ribbons were left hanging on the right for married women and on the left for the unmarried. Again, the *Krusstikije* (pleasant word!), strips of red baize hanging from their velvet collars, were worn on the right by the married and on the left by the virgins of this seafaring town. But it was the long coat or dressing gown, the *wenkte,* of flowered chintz that was the beauty of their costume, of glorious abstract 'Indian' design. The younger girl, sitting in the painted sledge, wears a short coat of blue and purple flowered chintz, to show she is in slight mourning; she, also, has a fichu of checked Indian cotton, and these indefatigable gatherers of information tell us that two hundred different patterns of the checked cottons could be recognized. And that petticoats, three in number, would be the correct costume for that winter day!

The elderly lady and gentleman of another illustration are not less entrancing; he, for his three-cornered hat, black breeches and stockings, and waistcoat of pale blue and silver damask. The old lady wears a blue and white striped cap in the shape of those worn at Volendam; but not so fast, it is tilted forward, not put straight on the head. In the island of Schokland* when that was inhabited, before the fishermen of that salt strand were transhipped to Volendam, these hats were worn straight upon the head, while in Volendam they were tilted back a little. The old lady is in mourning. That is why her *zondoek* or hat scarf is of blue and white. In Hindeloopen there were seven shades of mourning, from full black, through dark blue Indian cotton with a thin white check, dark blue with broader white, to white with thin stripes of dark blue. And this old couple have attained to the third out of these seven degrees of mourning. The old lady wears a *wenkte* or long dressing gown of superb red and blue and purple in a magnificent design. Her corset laces should be green and not dark blue, as in the deeper shades of mourning. Even the painted wooden reading desk, with a Bible on it, is in blue and white to show they are in mourning.

The two other plates of Hindeloopen costume show us a babe in swaddling clothes, wearing a *slaapwenkte* or sleeping gown of figured blue Indian cotton, with one armhole only. But this unfortunate child, robed as though for the Antarctic blizzards, and enclosed in the same garments for many months on end, has sleeves of white chintz with flowers and leaves in red and green, and as

---

* Maaskamp in his book of Dutch costumes (1798) refers, particularly, to the Schoklanders, who, he says, still possess the secret 'to paint the hair gold yellow', as in the time of Tacitus; and referring to the woman in his plate he continues, quaintly, 'Even at present they are still so beautiful, as in Tacitus times, but their dress is strange. Behold here, the regimentals of a drummer, or the State-livery of a footman, provided with lace on all the seams.'

outer covering wears red Indian cotton with a pattern of blue flowers, one of the most satisfying of all the chintz designs. In the last plate we have a nurse and child. A little girl with cap, sleeves, bodice, and overskirt all of red and white checked Indian cotton, but each of these materials is of slightly different design, with varying degrees of thickness of the stripe or checking, and after looking at them for a little time we come to realize how there could be as many as 200 different patterns of checked cottons in the haberdashers' shops at Hindeloopen. And the nurse? She wears an apron like a long smock falling from her shoulders, and the traditional pattern of the tree of life is in the centre of this. But, we quote from the pair of authors, 'at a time when all other aprons were made with patterns round the edge only nurses wore this central device'.

But the dresses of this little town were, in reality, far more beautiful than they can be made to appear in any written description, or in a drawing. For proof of this it is only necessary to see the collection of dresses in the little Town Hall of Hindeloopen, one floor of which is turned into a small museum. Not only the chintzes and flowered or figured cottons, but the forms of the dresses are of surpassing beauty, and there can be no doubt that Hindeloopen must have been one of the most beautiful places in the world for costume and that its name should be upon the lips of all designers of textiles and stage artists. There is as much to be learned here, in little, as in the wonderful Musée des Tissus at Lyon.

Was Hindeloopen, with its 1,000 inhabitants, alone in the world? No, it had a 'suburb'. Indeed, the drawing of the unmistakable Hindeloopen costume in Maaskamp has the name beneath, misspelt, of Molkwerum. This small village, a Dutch league from Hindeloopen, was described to Havard, for no apparent reason, as the 'labyrinth of Friesland'. In his day it had a population of but 300 persons. The author of *Les Délices du Pays Bas* started the legend by stating that 'if a stranger enters this village he must secure a guide to enable him to get out of the labyrinth'. Formerly, Havard remarks, the language and costume of both 'cities' was the same; he detected a difference, being a Frenchman, in the shade and manner of folding the *zondoek* or turban, and noted that the women of Molkwerum did not wear the cloak or cape (the *wenkte*?) of the Hindeloopen ladies. But Havard made one important minor discovery, Molkwerum, contained, he said, 220 Calvinists, 70 Mennonites, 11 Catholics, and two Lutherans. Seventy Mennonites was, to the total population, then, as one in three. Now turn to what he says of Hindeloopen, that 'out of 200 houses remaining of the old town, 50 or 60 were built on the same plan, having the same frontage and apertures and placed side by side in the same spot'. It is the same proportion, one in three. It is to be inferred that one-third of the inhabitants of Hindeloopen were Mennonites. This we believe to be the truth, and that it is an explanation, in part, of the wealth of the Hindeloopers, but we forbear to number with them that enchanting pair of maidens of Molkwerum portrayed in *The National Costumes of Holland* and described by ourselves at an earlier page, the pair of young girls wearing 'toppers', one of hatter's plush trimmed with gold galon and green silk fringe, the other in a tall straw 'topper' trimmed with brown and green ribbons, and carrying a basket of fresh strawberries in her hand. Those could not be Mennonites. It is hard to forget their Frisian fair hair and blue eyes, the golden rosettes on their foreheads, the flounces of lace framing their faces, and above all, that pair of 'toppers'.

Who and what were the Mennonites? It is a question most appropriate to this part of Holland and will lead us into bypaths as winding as any in the 'labyrinth of Friesland'. Side tracks they may be, but the experienced voyager in art and history may long as much as the modern motorist to leave the main road and enjoy the country. It may seem in the beginning to be a goose chase, as it might be to devote time and labour to the Muggletonians.* But the Mennonites are far more interesting, and Menno Simonsz, their founder, was born in Friesland in 1496 at Witmarsum near Franeker. He was ordained a Catholic priest, but was soon in unarmed rebellion against the Roman Church. For Menno Simonsz

---

* Followers of Ludovic Muggleton, a journeyman tailor in the reign of Charles II. A small remnant of the sect was still found in England in the middle of last century.

was a passive Anabaptist and expressed pious horror at the excesses practised in the New Jerusalem at Münster. This is not the place to enter into that curious and bloodstained history, and we will only say that high up on the tower of St Lambert's Church in that old city still hangs, or were hanging, till the entire town was battered and 'blitzed' down, the three iron cages in which the bodies of the Anabaptists, John of Leyden, Krechting and Knipperdollinck, their leaders, were exposed after being torn with red-hot pincers. John of Leyden, roaring like a bull, bit through the rope and had to be bound to the stake with an iron collar. The siege and punishment of Münster was, typically, a Teutonic horror. But the career of Menno Simonsz, though dangerous, was set along more peaceful ways.

He preached in Friesland and set an example to his followers. His doctrine was complete pacifism and on the whole, but for a few incidents, he was left in peace. Nevertheless, upon occasion, he escaped narrowly and by exercising his native wits. For instance, one day he was travelling, when the Spaniards had put a price upon his head, in a closed wagon which was a public conveyance, like the modern bus or tram, running between Franeker and Leeuwarden. At a point upon the road the wagon was stopped by Spanish soldiers and the officer coming up to the door enquired of Menno, who was sitting next to it : 'Whether Menno Simonsz was amongst them?' Menno, turning to the other travellers, repeated the question and they all answered 'No!' Then, addressing the Spaniard himself, Menno said : 'They say that Menno Simonsz is not among us,' and the Spaniard went away.* In the end, seeking peace above all else, Menno Simonsz withdrew from Friesland, and accepting the hospitality of a German nobleman

* I am reminded of a story, a 'period piece' told me by my father. He was four years old, in 1864, and looking for his sister. His mother was in the room wearing a large crinoline, and though he did not know it his sister had crawled under that and was hiding there. To his question, 'Where is Florence?' his mother answered, looking down: 'I cannot see her.' Such answers, a Dutch friend tells us, are still known in Holland as Mennonite lies; but my grandmother, at all costs, even in a little children's game, had told the truth, and this was all that mattered to a pietistic mid-Victorian.

went to live, and die, in a little town between Lübeck and Hamburg. By a generation after his death the followers of his doctrine had much increased in number. So had the Anabaptists generally, for the *Annales Anabaptistici*, a forbidding compilation, enumerates 77 different sects all holding the same common principles, but varying in opinions. And it was not long before there were dissensions among the Mennonites.

The dispute arose over the question of excommunication, not Papal but social, for the argument concerning the putting into Coventry, as we would call it, vulgarly, or depriving sinners and transgressors of all social intercourse with even their nearest, and not necessarily their dearest, of relations. The Mennonites split at once into two bodies, *die Fienen* (the Fine) and *die Groben* (the Coarse), though the niceties of these terms may be lost upon us. *Die Groben* (the Coarse), it is interesting to learn, inhabited chiefly the Waterland in North Holland, and were known, therefore, as Waterlanders, primitive inhabitants, in fact, of Broek, that neurotically clean village, and of the most odd and curious isle of Marken. The other body of Mennonites, *die Fienen* (the Fine), lived in Flanders and were known as Flandrians or Flemings. Then the Flandrians quarrelled among themselves and the Fine Mennonites became known, respectively, as Flandrians and Frieslanders. But they joined forces again over some obscure point of argument. The Flandrians, Frieslanders, and Germans became merged into the Waterlanders; while the others, incalcitrant and few in number, only three congregations in all Holland in the middle of last century, were, simply, old Fleming Baptists. But the dissensions of the Mennonites were not yet ended. In the middle of the seventeenth century a body of those living in Friesland broke off from the community and called themselves Olckewallists from the name of their leader, and went the length of being prepared to hope for the final salvation of Iscariot. Finally, and this is confusing, the Fleming church of Amsterdam broke into two bodies in 1664, calling themselves Galenists and Apostoolians, and then the Waterlanders united with the Galenists, but refused to take the name of Mennonites.

The doctrines of the Mennonites included non-resistance, non-swearing of oaths, non-participation in civil government, non-belief in infant baptism, seclusion from the world and, later, resistance to military conscription. They numbered many converts in Switzerland and Germany and Alsace, and one of their strongholds was in Amsterdam, a city which had become a refuge, in any case, for Anabaptists from the fall of Münster onwards. We are not to suppose that, at first, they differed from others in appearance, though in Germany early in the sixteenth century the Anabaptists fasted and practised other austerities, and dressed in coarse garments, and with long beards, wandered preaching round the countryside. Rembrandt, at any rate, painted the double portrait of Anslo the Mennonite preacher and his wife, and portraits, too, of other Mennonites, though there is nothing distinctive in their clothes or features. Rembrandt is even supposed to have been a Mennonite himself, but this is probably untrue. But the peculiarities of the sect became apparent later, when they retained the costume of their forefathers and became fixed and old-fashioned in their ways. We would expect, therefore, to find them at their most peculiar development in the eighteenth century, and we should be correct.

The isolated communities of Mennonites in Friesland and in Groningen had attained great wealth, more particularly in the northern part of the latter province lying between the capital and the North Sea, districts which are little known to this day, but have been described to the present writer as wooded, with great cornlands, too, and as fertile and beautiful as that part of Holland between Amersfoort and Arnhem, the great region for Dutch country houses. It was the careful habits of the Mennonites which made them rich : 'reciprocal charity, severity of manners and love of labour'. Not that the neighbouring farmers were any poorer, for this was the Arcadia of the rich peasants, and so it continued until the middle of the nineteenth century, when the impressionable de Amicis, whom we summon once more to our assistance, could see such a spectacle as a nuptial procession of peasants, more than 30 carriages, all with shell-shaped bodies, covered with gilding and painted flowers, and drawn by the robust, black Frisian horses. In each carriage sat a peasant in his gala costume with a woman at his side in golden casque and white lace veil. 'The horses went at a quick trot, the women clung each to her companion's arm and their casques glittered in the light.' De Amicis says that, 'throwing sugar plums to the crowd, the cortège passed by and disappeared like some fantastic vision in the midst of festive shouts and laughter'. The Mennonites in their broadcloth and wide-brimmed hats will have been watching this, not so much, perhaps, like skeletons as like lay figures at the feast.

It would seem scarcely credible that those Puritans should still be visible in the modern world, but they exist, unaltered, as the Pennsylvania Dutch settlers, and a glimpse of them, helped by an article in *The National Geographic Magazine*,* will enable us to follow up the later convolutions of the Mennonites. For in Holland, in Friesland especially, there are still Mennonites but they look like anyone else. It is in Lancaster County, Pennsylvania, that they still look different from others. But sectarian complications had begun again amongst the Mennonites. At the end of the seventeenth century, Jacob Amen, a Swiss Mennonite, tried to return to the first principles of Menno Simonsz, and his followers were called the Amish. A group of them settled at Salm in Alsace and employed in agriculture, wore a peculiar dress, used 'hooks' and 'eyes' in place of buttons, and let their beards grow. Their women had loose hair until they married, when they bound it round their heads. This was the beginning of the controversy about 'hooks' and 'eyes', but soon the Amish who, meanwhile, had emigrated to Pennsylvania in 1683 and 1698, split into two bodies, the House Amish (Old Order) and Church Amish (New Order), the former body only holding their services in homes and barns. The House Amish to this day use only horsedrawn vehicles and scorn the telephone and electric light.

Sectarians were pouring from Northern Europe in Pennsylvania. The Schwenkfelders, originating in Silesia, but numbering many Dutchmen among them, appeared in 1734. Their founder

* For July 1941, in an article by Elmer C. Stauffer.

was Caspar Schwenkfeld von Ossing, a Silesian knight of the sixteenth century and counsellor to the Duke of Leignitz. His followers reached America by way of Denmark. And there were the Dunkers or Dunkards, German Baptists who had taken refuge in Holland, and in the Duchy of Cleves, and who reached America in 1719 with Johann Conrad Beissel, who founded a group that celebrated Saturday as the true Sabbath, and who was responsible for the foundation of the Cloister of Ephrata. This Society of the Solitary, of both sexes, established in one of the most beautiful early wooden buildings in the United States, was along Cocalico Creek. There were separate buildings for the men and women; the men adopted the dress of white friars, a long white robe reaching to the heels, a sash or girdle round the waist, and a cowl hanging down the neck. All who entered the Society received monastic names. Celibacy was recommended, but not enjoined; and such works as Bunyan's *Pilgrim's Progress* were printed in German at Ephrata. Unfortunately, this curious community soon collapsed, though the Cloister of Ephrata survives as a three-storey wooden building.

Of all the sectarian communities of America the Mennonites are the most interesting, for among the Amish of both Orders the costume of men and women has hardly altered from two centuries ago. Old Order Amish make almost everything they wear except their boots. Professional hatters, however, manufacture their black felt broadbrims, and the Amish women plait the rye straw for the hats that their menfolk wear in summer. The Amish are to be seen in the market towns of Lancaster County selling their produce, driving in horse-buggy, four-wheeled wagons, the men wearing beards and broadbrimmed hats and still with 'hooks' and 'eyes', not buttons, on their suits of sober black; the women in plain black cloaks and bonnets. They live in red brick farmhouses that have green shutters and snow-white paint and great Holstein barns. The furniture, china, rugs, and counterpanes of the Mennonites are much collected, as are their *fractur* paintings, coloured drawings upon deeds of birth, marriage, or baptism, and survivals of the ancient art of illumination. Fiinally, we cannot

forbear to mention the names of the apples that the Amish grow :
Rambos, Smokehouse, Winesaps, Tulpehockens. The last, surely
a memory of Holland, for *tulp* is the Dutch word for tulip.

And we return to Friesland; and to a community not less
curious, that of the Labadisten at Wieuwerd, in the flat plain not
far from Leeuwarden, but towards the lakes and meres. A very
little place, remote now, as it ever was, but the retreat, once, of
some remarkable and saintly persons, who found peace for their
souls in distant Friesland. They were not boors or peasants, and
their leaders were persons who had lived long in the world of
learning. The founder, Jean de la Badie, a Frenchman 'of decayed
noble family', born near Bordeaux, was educated as a Jesuit, was
expelled from that Order, joined the Reformed Church as a
minister, but began soon 'to propagate new and peculiar opinions'
of a mystical and impromptu nature, for it was his practice to
preach, extempore, for upwards of two hours, performances by
which his fire and energy gained many converts. The repute of this
voluble and energetic Gascon, whose character can be read in
the features of his portraits, spread far and wide in this age before
the cinema or other Sabbath entertainment. Jean de la Badie
was invited to London; and whether by invitation or no, he was
soon appointed minister to a London chapel. Next he moved to
Holland and was pastor of Middelburg, in Zeeland, a congenial
island setting, for in the words of an English Jesuit, 'it swarmed
with heretics and Anabaptists', and had lately been the centre
of the Brownists.* De la Badie could not let the local costumes pass

* Founded by Robert Brown, chaplain to the Lord-Treasurer Burghley,
but arrested and imprisoned on many occasions for 'the intemperate
language in which he spoke of the Church of England'. He fled to Holland
and opened a meeting house at Middelburg in 1588. A year or two after,
he returned home and through the influence of Lord Burghley obtained a
rectory in Northamptonshire, where, when upwards of eighty years of age,
he was carried to prison for an assault upon the parish constable and died
in Northampton jail in 1630, 'boasting', as Fuller reports, 'that he had
been committed to two-and-thirty prisons, in some of which he could not
see his hand at noon day'. The subsequent sub-history of this sect, their
split into Franciscan and Ainsworthian Brownists, and the application and
admission of the last six surviving members of the Amsterdam congrega-

uncensored. The peasant women of Walcheren, of which island Middelburg is capital, fortified by the seven petticoats, known as *keusen* or 'choices', which they wore on Sundays, had the daring habit not only of having bare arms, but of so tightening the sleeves above the elbows that their arms became reddened in colour, which was, and still is, the local criterion of beauty. De la Badie preached against this iniquity, recommending the use of *moffen* or woollen mittens, which to this day are known as *Labadisten*. After a few years, leaving, we may fear, this island paradise of the farmers a purer place than he found it, the fiery predicator removed his eloquence to Amsterdam.

But already he had welcomed a female convert not less celebrated than himself. This lady was the famous Anna Maria van Schuurman, a person of prodigious talents and true saintliness. Her home was at Utrecht, of which city she was chief ornament, for she corresponded, generally in Latin, with all the literati of her day, and though the meaning of this is lost upon us, 'was much applauded by the great Salmacius'. She knew French, German, Italian, and Spanish, of the living tongues, and Latin, Greek, Hebrew, and Ethiopian, in which language she wrote some poems. But, also, she was celebrated for her beauty. And she drew and painted. She was sculptor, etcher, and engraver. She painted her own portrait and those of several of her friends, and sculptured their busts. She modelled in wax; she etched and engraved her own portrait and made embroideries of flowers. She engraved, also, with a diamond point on glass, a minor art which Dutchmen of the time were bringing to perfection. She was famed as a poetess; distinguished visitors to Utrecht sought interviews with her, and if any criticisms can be made of this remarkable woman it is that she tried her hand at too many things and was not content with one or other of her talents. Early in her twenties she renounced the world and became an ardent follower of de la Badie, and it is evident that this saintly person entertained a love for him that

tion into the British Reformed or Presbyterian Church of that city, all is set forth, alphabetically, in *The Faiths of the World*, by the Rev. James Gardner, M.D. and A.M.

transcended mere affection. It was through her influence with the Princess Elizabeth, daughter of the Prince Palatine, her close friend, that the Labadists as they were called, already, found asylum at Herworden, in Westphalia. Thence they went to Altona, always a refuge for dissenters, where de la Badie died in 1674.

But, now, another friend came to the rescue, Cornelis van Aerssen, a nobleman who was three times Governor of Surinam. He offered the Labadists his castle of Waltha or Thetinga, near Wieuwerd, to which the community repaired, 300 or 400 in number, and built their houses round the castle walls. Here, Anna Maria van Schuurman wrote her *Eukleria,* a religious and mystical soliloquy; and to Wieuwerd came another convert hardly less celebrated in her day, Mevrouw Maria-Sibylla Merian, who abandoned her husband* and arrived with her mother and two daughters. This lady, who has the double distinction that she is mentioned in the dictionaries both of science and of painting, was a member of a famous family of artists. Being born in 1647, she was a generation younger than Anna Maria van Schuurman, and with regard to what has just been said, we note with interest that she had not long been married. At an early age she had gone, as a pupil, to Abraham Mignon, who painted fruit and flowers. This, too, was the direction taken by the talents of Anna Maria van Schuurman, but Maria-Sibylla painted flowers and insects particularly, and was the first person to observe the metamorphosis of butterflies. She had already published two collections of her engravings before she came to Wieuwerd; but her real fame is due to the two visits that she paid to Surinam, and that may be connected by more than coincidence with her sojourn in this Frisian castle belonging to the three-times governor of that remote colony. We must anticipate by quoting what she says in the preface to her magnificent *Dissertation sur les Insectes de Surinam,* wherein, alternatively in French and Latin, it is set forth that after her two earlier publications just mentioned, she set forth for Friesland and for Holland, mentioning the former, it will be noted, as a separate country, where she continued her examination of insects

---

* Johann Andreas Graff (1637–1701), a painter of Nuremberg.

and butterflies, but more particularly in Friesland, for in Holland she had not the opportunity of searching for them in the hedges and ditches, though she is ready to admit that the curious repaired this defect by bringing her caterpillars so that she could study their metamorphoses. Nothing, however, that she saw in Holland was more curious than the cabinets of insects brought there from the two Indies, creatures of which none knew either the origin or the means of generation, which is to say, how the caterpillars were transformed into chrysalises and their other changes. It was this that resolved her to undertake the long and difficult journey to Surinam, where she arrived in June 1701, and stayed there for two years, studying her subjects and making hundreds of careful coloured drawings upon vellum, 72 of which, later, formed the body of the great work in question. She was assisted in this task by her daughter, Johanna-Helena, who had accompanied her to Friesland, and who painted insects and flowers equally well with her mother. We learn that this daughter married to her mother's satisfaction a rich burgher of Surinam, a merchant named Herold,* and that Johanna-Helena came back with her husband a second time in order to complete the vellum paintings for her mother's book. It seems probable, for we must digress for a further moment—though any mention of Holland is a pleasant digression for an Englishman—that the governor Cornelis van Aerssen may have invited the Merians to Surinam. But, indeed, this part of South America, better known as Dutch Guiana, of which little is heard even now, had a most curious history. There was a moment when it nearly became a Jewish colony. Several families of Portuguese Jews had emigrated from Holland into Dutch Brazil, and when the Portuguese recovered that vast country, the Jews took refuge in Barbados, hence the old Jewish tombstones to be found there and in the Dutch West Indies. David Nassi, alias Joseph Nunes de Fonseca, and others, obtained a charter from the Dutch West India Company to establish a

---

* Can they have been related to the G. Herold who painted the *chinoiserie* scenes and figures upon early Meissen china? It seems not unlikely in such a pedigree of artists.

Jewish colony in Surinam, and Jews came there from Leghorn and other cities. They acquired great wealth and were big slave owners, and, in fact, slavery in Dutch Guiana was not abolished until 1856 and was attended with much cruelty.* This curious history is completed by the presence of great numbers of Moravians, totalling 29,917 Hernutes in 1930, if we are to trust the *Almanach de Gotha,* a reliable, if unlikely authority on this sort of information. The Herrnhutters, as it is spelt more generally, derive their name 'The Lord's Watch' from a passage in the 84th Psalm : 'to watch the door in the house of my God'. Their origin was in the fifteenth century, for they were Hussites or early Protestants from Hungary and Bohemia, in the first place, who professed the doctrines of the Confession of Augsburg. They fled for refuge from the Jesuits of Bohemia to the estates of Count Zinzendorf in Saxony, where they built their village of Herrnhut. It consisted of neat rows of little houses or cottages, and the orderliness of their lives was displayed in their women's costume distinguished by differently coloured ribbons. The girls wore deep red; unmarried women pink; married blue; and widows grey or white. Such were their settlements throughout Europe and in America; for instance, at Sarepta upon the steppe road to Astrakhan, there was a flourishing colony of Hernutes,† who prematurely conducted their affairs upon purely communistic principles, kept a shop and

* The first Portuguese Jews arrived in Curaçao in 1651 from Holland, and from Brazil under Geosuah de Mordechay Henriques in 1654. In 1692 they built a synagogue in Willemstad, the capital of the island, their rabbi becoming, later, rabbi of the old synagogue in Kingston, Jamaica. The Curaçao synagogue is stated to be a replica of that of the Portuguese Jews in Amsterdam and must resemble, therefore, that of Bevis Marks in London.

The writer visited Willemstad in 1965 long after this footnote was written. It does indeed much resemble the Bevis Marks synagogue in Aldgate with its splendid *hechals* or cupboards of jacaranda wood, and shining brass chandeliers. But it has this one difference, it has a sanded floor.

† Care must be taken not to confuse the Hernutes with the Hutterites, Moravian Anabaptists of sixteenth-century origin who still possess communities in remote parts of the United States and Canada, *e.g.*, upon Hudson Bay, where they live in community by manual labour.

warehouse for their products in St Petersburg, and were famed for Sarepta mustard throughout Tsarist Russia. We read, too, that 'with the view of increasing the population, colonies of Mennonites from Holland and Prussia were established in the heart of the country of the Zaporogian Cossacks', near the Sea of Azof, 'but that they have lately', in 1875, 'shown a tendency to emigrate to America in order to avoid military conscription'. Descendants of many of these, it is probable, are living with the Dunkards and the Amish in Lancaster County among the Pennsylvania Dutch settlers.

The Labadists at Wieuwerd lived after the pattern of these lay ascetics. Their doctrines approached most nearly those of the Schwenkfelders, who recognized the gifts of prophecy and internal revelation. Anna Maria van Schuurman lived among them for the last few years of her life, and relics of her handiwork are preserved, as we have seen, at Franeker and also at Wieuwerd. In the crypt of the church there, four mummied bodies are shown in their coffins, supposed Labadists, one of whom, we hope wrongly, is said to be this learned and saintly person, for it is not pleasant to think that such an artist and poetess is exposed to public gaze. But it is not certain that any of the four are Labadists. It is only that the sojourn of the sect in Wieuwerd is the sole, and tenuous, claim of this remote village to a share of fame. The community was visited by Locke when it had been at Wieuwerd for nine years, and contrary to other reports, he estimated that it contained 80 to 100 inmates. This was the very time, probably, in which Maria-Sibylla Merian was amongst the adepts, and from their identity of interests she has become confused in some minds with Anna Maria van Schuurman; for the editor of the life of Dr Edmund Calamy (how fine a name for a religious controversialist!) tells us that 'there is in the British Museum a volume of drawings by this lady, beautifully coloured, to represent the natural history of Surinam'. The Labadists, says Locke, 'receive all ages, sexes and degrees upon examination and trial, and live all in common', and we have to regard life there as something of a metaphysical conceit, for this is the century of Port-Royal and Little Gidding, and it is no surprise to find among its members and correspondents such persons as 'mystical' chemists and astrologers . The Labadists of Wieuwerd died out, however, in a generation, and it is said that by 1717 the community was extinct. Surviving memory, those mummied bodies apart, would seem to be confined to a strong frieze cloth still sold in Friesland as Labadist cloth. It is the more curious, therefore, to be told on the authority of *The Dictionary of Religious Thought and Ethics* that only 20 years ago Wieuwerd was still visited, annually, by a few Labadists, so that there are persons living somewhere who still recall the printing and weaving, the fruit culture and bee-keeping, and the spiritual and metaphysical exercises once practised in this remote place.*

The moment now approaches when we have to depart from this beautiful and lovely Friesland, probably for ever, and there could be no picture of it to last longer in the mind than that interminable stretch along the top of the dyke, called euphoniously, the Lemster Hop, and traversed upon the return journey on a blazing July day after a vain attempt to cross the new polder to the magical and ever elusive isle of Urk that lies out in the middle of the Zuyder Zee. Upon the way thither we had been through Heerenveen to the Oranje Woud, lovely for its long canals and formal woods, and representing with more truth than is usual to these guide book *clichés,* 'a sort of little Versailles of Friesland', for it was created out of a peat bog by Albertine-Agnes, widow of the Stadhouder Willem Frederik of Nassau. The 'palaces' in this bucolic province are little pretty country houses, but the groves and avenues of the Oranje Woud are worthy of the great age of formal gardens. The Lemster Hop is incredible in contrast, and the

* It is amusing to find in *Choix de Coquillages et de Crustaces* by F. M. Regenfuss, Copenhagen, 1758, the great work on conchology, with coloured plates, which is probably the most beautiful of all Danish books, that a particular kind of shell from the Iles Frédéricienne (Danish East Indies) was called the Drole de Beguines, and the author adds: 'Les Beguines étoient une secte de Réligieuses Hérétiques. . . . On connoit encore à present en Hollande des filles sous ce nom que jouissent de certains bénéfices. La coeffure singulière que portent ces Beguines a donné lieu à la denomination de Begynedrolen (Droles de Beguines).'

16   Volendam

17   *Traditional interior in Staphorst*

appalling road surface quadruples the distances and makes the cultivated desolation as tremendous as the Gobi desert. Great farms a mile or so apart, with rough tracks leading to them; and below us, on the other side of the dyke, the new polder, treeless, nearly without houses, and stretching out of sight. The Russian Steppe, the deserts of Central Australia, the great plain stretching to the Rocky Mountains, these could not give stranger effects of immensity and loneliness. A few hours were like a lifetime on the Lemster Hop. There are families living 20 or 30 miles from anywhere out in the new polder, for it lies as far as Urk, leaving that island with the sea on one side, and with a land connection on the other, but more, not less, inaccessible for that fact. After a few hours of this road, the little coast town of Lemmer seems as bright and gay as Paris.

Last, or nearly at the end, for there are one or two digressions yet, comes the question of the Friesland cuckoo clocks, country relics, we like to think, of the great age of the clockmakers and silversmiths in Leeuwarden. The painted wooden cuckoo clocks are to be seen all over Friesland, more often without the cuckoos, and they form a minor art as fascinating as the painted street carts of Palermo, usually with painted cupids and garlands of fruit and flowers. They are the equivalent of our English folk art of merry-go-rounds, of Gypsy caravans and painted canal barges. There were celebrated makers of these clocks at Loure, and such clocks are still made in that little town and are not unworthy of their past. But we had no time to go there; neither did we visit Ijlst, a little town which figures enchantingly in Doughty's old books about the Friesland meres, where he mentions its painted houses with green shutters and its aspect of a Chinese town upon the Imperial canal; the latter half of this phrase is our own invention, but we have no doubt it is what he intended though he may never have heard of the Imperial canal. But it is apparent from his description that Ijlst is, or was, something of a Broek-in-Waterland transferred to Friesland, and we leave it with an imaginary picture in our minds of children, and even stolid, elderly Dutchmen, flying kites above those shining roofs, many pairs of swans upon the still canals, and little boats to take you anywhere, or nowhere, tied up before the painted doors.

But we conclude with the painted biers of Workum, minor works of art that we would never have seen, owing to the impenetrability of Dutch churches and the hopeless task of asking for the key, but that one aisle of this church had collapsed and it was possible to climb through the scaffolding and get inside. Workum is a little 'dead' town half-way from Makkum to Hindeloopen. It was to be feared that the painted biers would have been removed when the roof fell in and been locked up for months or years, but there they were, piled up on top of one another and looking in that moment like the stretchers waiting ready for an air-raid warning. There are eight of them with long poles or handles to be carried by twice as many men; one bier each for the different guilds or professions; for doctors, or apothecaries, seamen, builders, farmers, silversmiths, for children and, it is said, though denied, for suicides. Each of these biers has its sides painted with appropriate scenes; little 'peasant' paintings dating from the middle of the eighteenth century, of the same quality as the better Swedish 'peasant' paintings and offering a most lifelike rendering not less accurate because *naïf* and awkward, of what daily life must have been in Workum some 200 years ago. These paintings are works of art, decidedly, and to be preferred to the para-Victorian, smooth finish of many famous pictures in the Dutch galleries. The building scene upon the guild of the builders or bricklayers shows us an old Dutch town as it might have been depicted by 'Douanier' Rousseau or an Umbrian primitive; while the bier of the farmers has a picture of the Dutch polders that conveys their desolate yet, withal, tamed nature in a reality that can be discovered in no other painting. The church at Hindeloopen is reported to contain more examples of these painted biers, but this statement cannot be verified. All that is positive is that these paintings, of so strange a destination at Workum, are works of art, in little. They afford one more proof of the wonderful flowering of the lesser arts along the 'dead shores' of the Zuyder Zee and in Friesland, relics of a rustic Arcadia of inland waters and level meadows. Of its inhabitants with their fair hair and golden helmets, their painted rooms and town halls, their curious furniture and figured cotton dresses, we have written at some length. But Friesland is a land apart, and for all its lack of hills and running water, as rich in lesser works of art as the more favoured shores of Italy and Spain. We will end, not inappropriately, with an old story. It concerns a Spanish general who, one day, showed a Friesland peasant a ripe orange and said with pride : 'This is a fruit which my country produces twice a year!' It is de Amicis who tells the story. 'And this,' replied the peasant, producing a pound of fresh butter, 'is the fruit which my country produces twice a day.'

*   *   *

Note : It has been an interesting experience to visit Friesland again after such a lapse of time, and not be disappointed. How characteristic are its isolated farms here and there all over the low horizon in every direction, most of them now with television aerials and to some extent therefore in the contemporary world, though a Dutch friend told us of the Frisian recruits in her son's regiment and of how much they suffered from home-sickness and longed to be back upon their farms, despite which they were among the best soldiers in the Dutch army, or so we were informed.

Leeuwarden proved as fascinatingly remote yet near, as before, though I have to cool down my rhapsody upon the painted room in the Coulon House (see p. 97) which I found to be about a quarter the size I remembered it to be, though certainly still beautiful and part and parcel of the Dutch East Indian dream. But the reader is asked to remember this was written in the post-war euphoria of the summer of 1947, in which the Dutch were fully participant, and no wonder! I would not, however, want to detract by a single word from my admiration for the Frisian Museum in Leeuwarden which is an utter and entire delight. But particularly its upper floor, arrival at which in midst of a crowd of school children playing a game of 'hide and seek' upon the stair remains a cheerful and happy memory.

The pair of portraits of patrician ladies wearing the immense

Deutsche muts or cartwheel hats which I recalled from the farther room at the Coulon House, and which had been the complement to that former experience, were missing. No one indeed remembered them. And what would there be waiting up the noisy and even dangerous stair? But one need not have worried. The Frisian and Hindeloopen painted rooms and the show cases full of Frisian costumes are there in full extreme of fantasy. Nothing could be at once more graceful or more extraordinary than the model of a lady in the *Deutsche muts*! What would I not give to have been able to see some six or eight of these ladies coming out from church upon a Sunday morning and processing down the village, or, rather, small town street upon the Zuyder Zee! 'Friesland, we have to think, owing to its isolated situation – there was no causeway to Noord Holland, then, and in the east Friesland was bordered by marshes – its civilization has always had a special character.' So it is stated in a foreword to the guide for the Frisian Museum, and this is no less than true. But it is the diversity in their costumes and in the interiors of their houses that is so astonishing. What a difference between Workum, Stavoren, and the more famous Hindeloopen, all three of them small towns on the inland sea with never more than a few hundreds, or, at most, 2,000 to 3,000 inhabitants; but all busy – and so much more successfully busy! – at devising their own costumes and decorating distinctively their own dwellings than any 'art village' there has ever been! It is a phenomenon that has not been satisfactorily explained, and that in its own way is just as remarkable and strange as life in San Gimignano, Gubbio, or other Italian hill town in their fifteenth century or 'golden age'. That in the Netherlands it was the result of some sort of opiate dream of the East Indies, may be a near approach or approximation to the secret.

7. Two Excursions

I. *Sunday at Staphorst*

Coming down from Friesland the long way round, which is to
say along the south shore of what used to be the Zuyder Zee,
there is opportunity to witness one of the most extraordinary sights
to be seen in Holland. This, only if it is upon a Sunday morning,
which betrays the secret. For it must be a procession of people
leaving church. It is in Overyssel, a Dutch province that is not particularly interesting, and at a point where Holland is but a province wide, and there are only some 25 miles between the frontier
of Hanover and the Zuyder Zee. The two towns of any importance are Kampen and Zwolle. Kampen, where the Yssel, a
branch of the great Rhine, flows into the inland sea, is an old
town with an ancient church and a town hall with a too
elaborately carved sixteenth-century stone mantelpiece (I am
so muddled now, after reading Miss Nancy Mitford that I forget
if I should write fireplace or mantelpiece), but the lion of
Kampen is the Koornmarktspoort, a *donjon* or town gateway of
the early fourteenth century with two towers and hooded octagonal roofs recalling the great gateway of the old Seraglio at Istanbul
which was, in fact, the Sublime Porte. It is the gateway, but without the janissaries, and with stalls of melons and cheeses instead
of piles of heads. Zwolle is less, not more, interesting than Kampen.
There is a Gothic room in the town hall, and a gigantic wooden
Jacobean pulpit, a temple of Solomon for richness, in the church.
For the rest, Zwolle has some old houses and a few pretty street

pumps, stone objects in which it might be thought to be impossible to express the graces of the eighteenth century and the sillinesses of the age of Louis xv but, somehow, this has been achieved. Henri Havard, writing of Zwolle, says that 'it possesses large streets and pretty squares, which give it – pardon the expression – a very saucy look', but the only personal contact with this sauciness, during a previous visit, is the memory of a night spent between damp sheets.

Northward lies Drenthe, the heath or sandy waste of the Dutch boors, a dreary and desolate part of Holland, though this aspect of it may not be apparent to those persons for whom this is their home. There are some country houses; but the antiquities of Drenthe are antediluvian and take the form of tumuli or *Hunnebedden* (giants' graves), of great boulders that came here, involuntarily, by glacier, from Norway. Underneath them, for the men of the Stone Age rolled them into place, have been found wooden drinking vessels and stone axe heads, but no trace of iron. There are Dutchmen to whom Drenthe is the most typical part of Holland, for the landscape is natural, not artificial, a devotion which is that of the Irish to their peat bogs, for this province is one great peat bed, though without the mountains that give poetry to the Bog of Allen. Here, all is wild dreariness and the long desolate moorland, and the manners of the inhabitants were as rude and vigorous as the winds and rain, for at the village fairs or *kermissen* they used to fight with knives. The practice, which reads like an account of a wild night with the Foreign Legion in Sidi bel Abbes or Ksar es Souk, was for the boor who desired a fight to lay his clasp knife with the blade open on the table of the public house. This was the challenge, and anyone who touched it, drunk or sober, had to take out his knife and fight. Such circumstances give reason to the superstitious teetotalism of the stricter Calvinists, and it is an interesting thought that the Stone Age men of the giants' graves were innocent of this pastime, because they lived before the invention of intoxicating liquors.*

* Compare, also, the shin-kicking contests of Chipping Campden and the Cotswolds; in our homeland that is the muddied mother of rugby and

We have thought it necessary to draw this picture of the heaths of Drenthe, because it is in such contrast to Friesland, and we would infer, not having been there, to the rich farms of Groningen, a cornland, for it is agricultural not pastoral, that to our imagination should stretch all the way to Denmark, with delights of costume and of the lesser arts that in default of their existence we may like to think of for ourselves, and indeed, now in the mood, feel more than capable of describing. But the village to which we are journeying upon this Sunday morning is in the province of Overyssel, though but a mile or two from Drenthe. And it possesses this characteristic of Drenthe that it has nothing of the picturesque to recommend it. There could hardly be a more unlikely setting for a spectacle as peculiar as anything to be seen in Europe.

Upon the way there we were led astray to Giethoorn. This village, the name of which means what it nearly says in English, 'goat horn', has the reputation of being a modern Broek-in-Waterland. That is to say, it is 'quaint' as that term appeals to modern taste, 'a fairy water village' is a favourite description, and to the suburbia of trough gardens and villa rockeries it occupies the same position as Broek did 100 years ago to a world that was not tired yet of formal beds and topiary. It was to Giethoorn that all Dutchmen would direct our steps, counselling that three hours at least should be spent there, or even the whole day, reclining in a punt.

The village lies in marshes near the inland sea, and perhaps the beauty of Giethoorn is that the road ends and it is a cul-de-sac. You can go no farther; and if not willing to step down into a little boat have no other course than to follow a winding path along a wooden fence below deep-arching trees, with no sign of houses yet, till it turns another corner and we are in the pygmy water village, shaded as in a forest, and with every wooden cabin having its own high bridge of timber over the green water to the cabin opposite. The bridges are tall so as to allow the boats to pass beneath them, and 10 or more of the bridges can be seen in both

---

soccer football!! Till the middle of last century contestants would have their shins hammered by a friend, in practice, with a heavy wooden stave.

directions, but not more than a few of the houses owing to the over-
hanging trees. The houses are neither new nor old and are all built
to the same pattern. But Giethoorn is lacking in what was unique
at Broek, for the villagers of the Waterland could never have
allowed the weeds and green scum that clog the streams. Perhaps
it is this uncleanliness, so rare in Holland, that appeals to Dutchmen. The boats piled high with vegetables are poled along the
sluggish waters, and Giethoorn is like a little maze of flooded
ditches, all at right angles to each other. Were it not for the human
dwellings these would be ideal for crayfish streams. It must,
indeed, somewhat resemble a 'fairy water village' upon a winter
evening when the boughs are leafless and lights are showing in the
doors and windows. It must have been beautiful, too, a few hours
earlier upon this summer morning, before there was any sound of
human beings. Giethoorn is entertainment for children and it palls
in a few moments.*

But the serious and solemn Sabbath at Staphorst is but a few
miles away. Perhaps there is nothing like this anywhere else in
the world today. It is a long straggling village street lying upon
both sides of the main road from Meppel to Zwolle. This only
makes it more improbable, for there are garages, petrol pumps, and
all the noise and fumes of 'progress'. When you leave the main
road for the village street there is no one in sight. They are all in
church. We had been told that 11 o'clock upon Sunday morning
was the hour to be in Staphorst and been warned that it would
be better to leave the car in a lane and walk away. The inhabitants
resent strangers, and do not look with favour upon motor cars,
particularly upon a Sunday. Luckily our arrival was in time, for
the double village of Staphorst and Rouveen extends for at least
two miles and there was no one to help us find the church. The
houses, here again, are all alike with doors and shutters painted
green, large prosperous dwellings and not peasants' cabins. But
all empty. The church is a red brick, mid-nineteenth-century

* It was upon the road to Giethoorn that we passed the only storks' nests
that we saw in Holland. These birds, sadly enough, have nearly departed
from the Netherlands except, (1973), I am told, in Groningen.

building of no interest at all, but with large windows through which it was possible to see the women's galleries upstairs, completely crowded, and to hear the half-familiar strains of Calvinist hymns. There were psalms and a sermon and then more hymns, and we could even see some children fidgeting on their chairs and their gaze straying towards the world outside the windows. Then, much shuffling of feet and pushing back of chair legs as the congregation stood up and joined in singing the last hymn.

At about this moment a small procession came walking down a side-lane into the village street. They had come from a little chapel where the service ended earlier than in the big church, and they consisted chiefly of young girls dressed, uniformly, in dark blues and blacks, wearing some kind of bonnet, the original of which must have had an ostrich feather trimming. They began walking to their homes, and it was impossible to avoid a horrid feeling that we had come to the wrong end of the village, that this was not the parish church of Staphorst, and that we had missed the procession. What if the congregation whom we could hear singing those half-familiar hymns should prove to be Roman Catholics and not the men and women whom we had come long miles to see? The Calvinists, for all we knew, might live in Rouveen, the other half of Staphorst. And we were never able to find out who were the young girls we saw dressed in blue and black. They had been to the service in that little chapel and were probably some separate community living in Staphorst. For they were dressed quite differently from the others; perhaps they are members of the Dutch Reformed Church* or Old Catholics (Jansenists); but the church doors were flung open, with much noise and trampling the congregation came pouring out, and the procession formed. There are persons who have witnessed this Sunday march of the

* The Dutch Reformed Church (*Nederlandsch Hervormde Kerk*) comprises more than half of the population of Staphorst, as, also, of Spakenburg. A new, more severe Reformed Church (*Gereformeerde Kerk*) arose in the nineteenth century. Dr Ozinga informs us that the Lutherans in Holland are nearly always of German origin and that we would be, therefore, incorrect in referring to the Staphorsters as Lutherans. They could, more properly, be described as Calvinists.

inhabitants of Staphorst back from church who assert that the men come first, and that not until the last of the men has disappeared into his home do the women assemble into their battalion and march away. Such was not our experience. There was a pause of a few moments while they were dressing ranks, and then the women came by in columns of threes, in strict military formation.

Several features mark out this procession as being unique among church parades. There is no music, but they march in step. The tread of 'the monstrous regiment of women', though their cohorts, surely, would pass the censure of John Knox's cold blue, Covenanting eyes, is identical with that of all the other women in the procession. They all walk in the same attitude. Their heads are all bowed at the same angle and they all look upon the ground. For this alone it is unlike all other church parades. The women have no wish to be seen for themselves, but only as having given testimony in a body, and now returning to their homes. Not only do they stride with the same length of step, but their necks and shoulders are identical in manner of stooping, as though they have a heavy, invisible weight upon their backs. There is a curious padded effect about their waists and all are wearing identical silver buckled shoes.

When we recover from the first astonishment and look at them more closely, for which there is opportunity, for there are several hundreds of the women, and already, their column fills the village street for as far ahead as we can see, it is to notice that all carry their overcoats neatly folded, as though by military order, upon their left arms. And all, of course, are dressed alike, but with subtle differences of age and rank. Physically, too, they closely resemble one another. But, in fact, their curious walk is conditioned entirely by the clothes they wear. The *oorijzer* (gold, or in this case, silver headdress) as worn at Staphorst covers their ears and deafens them, which is the reason why they look upon the ground. It must make it difficult for them to move their heads. They can see; but their other senses are confined, as it might be, in blinkers and a tight snaffle rein. Their bodies are padded, also, on their hips and shoulders, and they are imprisoned in multiple petticoats so that they appear to have no waists. There is something military, not only in their walk and in the way they hold their arms, not swinging them for as we shall discover they are carrying weapons in their right hands, but, also, in the folding of their shawls, which is done as precisely as if to military regulations. Looking down their ranks as they march past, row after row, all alike and ageless, we would expect to see the heavy infantrymen's packs upon their shoulders.

The 'marching order' of the women of Staphorst is as follows : black sateen caps, stuffed with horsehair or paper, with two pairs of black satin ribbons, one to keep the *oorijzer* in position, and the other tied in a butterfly bow under their chins; and caps of white lace that make the black cap invisible and hide their hair. We continue; the plates or earflaps of the silver *oorijzer*, like silver discs upon their cheeks and, indeed, covering as though trepanning their entire skulls, but we only see the edges of the *oorijzer* and it ends with a curious corkscrew, spiral ornament pointing upwards so that this regiment of marching women appear to have a pair of silver antennae trembling at either nostril; ribbons of both caps, black and white, tied under their chins; red and white checked shawls of Frisian cotton, neatly folded and tucked into their waists; chest protectors or *kraplapen* of flowered cotton, like a breastplate front and back, with bright blue ribbons tied in a series of bows upon the waist; full skirts and bodices of black, home woven cloth and, it is surmised, red baize petticoats much padded on the hips. We pause here, for some of the women are wearing skirts and bodices of *vijfschaft*, woven from the wool of their own sheep and striped dark blue and black, and it is this material which the young girls wore whom we saw earlier, coming from the chapel. And we resume; flat-heeled shoes with silver buckles, and this is the tremendous feature of the Staphorst Sabbath, it is their weapon, they carry in their right hands Bibles with silver clasps upon long silver chains.

The solemn seriousness of this march of Calvinist women going back from church into their homes, dropping out individually as they pass their houses, never laughing or smiling, looking down upon the ground, is a spectacle of awe, not amusement, to the beholder. It has happened in recent years that ignorant and foolish onlookers who joked at this procession have been roughly handled by the Staphorsters, and it would be a brave person who displayed a camera. It is in their expression, when they deign to look at you, that they do so, disapproving. One of the young girls as she came past was crying. Had she been censured for fidgeting during prayers, or sleeping during the sermon? Draconian rules of conduct must govern all their lives. Perhaps an explanation of the extraordinary psychological stage of siege in such a community is to be found in reading of Dalecarlia in the eighteenth century, a province of Sweden abounding in great lakes and birchwoods. Here, in such villages as Leksand and Rättvik upon Lake Siljan, where there were sheds at the back of the church as shelter for the horses and even boathouses for those of the peasants who rowed across the lake, we read that the minister and village elders were empowered to levy fines upon those who deviated in the slightest degree from the minute regulations of costume, width of ribbon, shape of shoes, precise shape of the Dalecarlian peaked cap and so forth. At least, in Dalecarlia, they were remote and miles from anywhere. In Staphorst they are upon a main road; yet in *The National Costumes of Holland* we read of such minutiae as that in Rouveen, but only in Rouveen and not in Staphorst, the men wear a chin strap or 'stormband' to their hats, and the unmarried men a silver watch and chain on Sundays. There is, however, this in explanation, that as well as being strict Calvinists the population has inter-married and is much inbred. The strict rules are devised, as it were, to keep their thoughts from straying. And we read of other peculiar details, of how the little boys and girls up to three years of age are dressed alike, but for the boy's silver buttons on his cuffs; of how he is given two gold buttons on his shirt collar as soon as he can walk; of the waistcoats or *kamizools* worn by the older boys, of black beaver cloth with blue stitched buttonholes; of the silver *oorijzer* worn *over* the top of the *toet muts* or black sateen cap by the older girls, a most curious effect, and of their six undergarments; of the black sateen *nettes* or bonnets trimmed with silk fringe, and at one time with ostrich feather trimming with a rosette of black satin on the left and on the right side a clasp of silver filigree; and of the upper skirts of the young women kilted up to their waists to show their red baize petticoats, and of their working caps of gay flowered sateen.

While the women of Staphorst are still marching past, we wonder what can be the history of these 'peculiar people', for they are more a race apart than any mere religious community or sect. De Amicis, that Italian companion whom we dismissed with a farewell but who recurs again, has this to say of Staphorst : 'Beyond Meppel you enter the province of Overyssel and arrive in a short time at a village, if village it can be called, the strangest that the human mind can conceive. It consists of a row of rustic cottages with wooden fronts and thatched roofs, which succeed one another for the length of more than eight kilometres, planted each upon a narrow bank of earth which extends as far as the eye can see. The inhabitants of this village are the descendants of two ancient Frisian colonies who have religiously preserved the costume, manners, and traditions of their forefathers and live at ease on the produce of their lands. . . . The inhabitants are all Calvinists, sober, austere, and laborious. The men knit their own stockings in the intervals of time when not working in the fields; and such is their abhorrence of idleness that when they meet in council to deliberate upon the affairs of the village, each man brings his knitting in order not to have his hands unoccupied. They possess 6,000 hectares of land, divided into 900 zones or strips, about 5,000 yards in length and 30 in width.' And he adds that most of them can read or write, have a horse and eight or ten cows, never leave the village, and marry where they are born. De Amicis never mentions the Sunday church parade. It reads like the ancient Frisian or Saxon system of land tenure, and the inhabitants are said to speak a dialect of Frisian, *Boeren-Friesch* or peasant Frisian, so that we must conclude that they are of Frisian origin and have been intermarrying and fixing themselves in type for a minimum of 400 or 500 years. They seem to us a doomed race, on the next stage to becoming slow witted and moronic like the inhabitants of Marken, for it is impossible to believe that any outsider would marry into them. The Staphorsters only survive in virtue of their numbers, but are likely to become freakish and idiotic in another generation, not like the Volendammers, who will survive because their way of life is worth living. In common with the islanders of Urk and Marken, the Staphorsters have cut themselves off entirely from the outside world and must disappear in time.

Not, however, for so long as the elders of Staphorst can stay the siege. For the march of the regiment of women is nearly over. Bringing up the rear there appears, flanked on either side by an attendant, a tall old lady dressed in black wearing the golden skullcap or *oorijzer* of the Frisians and a black bonnet perched on top of that, the only aristocrat whom we saw who had kept to the golden headdress of the old noble ladies of Friesland, for the other casques, few in number, were all worn by peasants and old almshouse women. Who can she have been? Perhaps the wife of the minister;* but a vision, in any case, from a stricter and more solemn world. The last ranks are now marching past, and where the baggage wagons should come, after them, the men of Staphorst appear, soberly dressed in black, with black caps and short black coats cut like waistcoats. The Staphorsters in build are large, burly peasant farmers, looking with no kind eye at the spectator. There are, it is certain, not so many men as women in the procession, and here are the elders, the 'dominies' of Staphorst, last of the whole column.

To say that the three old men are forbidding in expression – using the present tense because today, while I write, is Thursday, and they will be coming out of church again in three days' time, on Sunday, along the rainy road of Staphorst – to call them dour and uncompromising towards the modern world would be as much a misunderstanding of the problems of life and death as it would

* The *Ouderlingen* (elders) are laymen; the 'dominie' is the minister; and we are informed that it is impossible that the wife of the 'dominie' should wear the national dress. This lady is probably, therefore, the wife of a small local landowner.

be to be found laughing with your hat on at a funeral. The centre figure of the three wears an ancient top hat, a long frock coat, and carries a Sabbatarian umbrella. As he passed there were contempt and fury in his gaze. Letting him precede us to a respectful distance, we followed in painful slowness, more than a little in awe, as who would not be of this figure from the universal past. After a few paces he turned to the right hand, and not looking back, walked slowly down a little garden to his front door, and went inside. Had we waited, we would have seen him come forth for the *Kesoatie,* the evening service, when the ranks are re-formed and the women carry psalm books instead of Bibles upon silver chains. But, in silence, we turned to find our car, and drove away.*

II. *Weekday at Spakenburg*

Upon an afternoon of high sailing summer clouds that menaced, but did not drop in rain, we took the road to Spakenburg, a little fishing town of which the delight and charm, for it has nothing else to offer, are its inhabitants. It has this, also, that it is only an hour by road from Amsterdam, in the province of Utrecht and upon the south shore of the Zuyder Zee. A delightful feeling of being nowhere – or anywhere – for in so short a time we shall be out of the world altogether, alone with ourselves and on a country lane that leads over fields and dykes to Spakenburg. A road that does not take you there directly, for the place is too unimportant; and the day of all days in which to watch the long shadows of the clouds upon the level country, for the Dutchmen, lacking mountains, have only the snowy shapes of cumulus and cirrus to throw a shade upon canal and polder. An afternoon that will be over too quickly, and that, this is another delight of it, can be upon any day of the week, and need not be a Sunday, for the

* The writer 'took tea', prosaically enough, on a weekday while passing Staphorst in April 1973. The children, he noted, are still in full costume, and the local customs, church parade included, are still little changed according to enquiry. For which reason, and in fear that like most things worth preserving they may be 'going going gone', this account is being reprinted,

Spakenburgers wear their best suits upon working days. They only do not put to sea on Sundays.

But we are no more than half-way to Spakenburg, in the wooded sandy country of the Gooi, spoiled by too many villas. By now, did we choose to deviate, we were within a mile or two of Weesp, which has a Stadhuis, in stone, built in the correct and chilly style of Louis XVI, one of the best examples of its kind in Holland, with much use of flat pilasters in the interior, finely chiselled mouldings and cornices, but none of the delightful absurdities of earlier and more bucolic days. And, again, if in the mood for it, there is Naarden, a little fortified town in the Vauban manner, only a few hundred yards from the main road, a place with tales of atrocities from Spanish times and, seen from the air, a matter of double salients of earth and water, star-shaped moats and ramparts, and an inner core with arrowheaded projectments, and every known device for covering fire. From the cockpit of an aeroplane? But we have to admit that, upon the ground, Naarden is very dull indeed and like a child's puzzle or an old toy fort.

Beautiful, shady woods begin, stretching much of the way to Amersfoort, and beyond, to Apeldoorn and William of Orange's palace of Het Loo, the sort of woods that bespeak royal hunting lodges, and here in confirmation is the summer palace of Soestdijk, a white building to which it is difficult to assign a date, for it belonged originally to William of Orange, our William III of Hampton Court, but was given by a grateful nation to the Prince of Orange who fought at Waterloo. It must be the second generation of beech trees; they are in full bough and not gnarled or broken. They make green tunnels of the asphalt roads and must be more lovely still when yellowing in autumn. A district of many hotels with gardens and rich villas, an air of comfortable prosperity, of summer holidays, of golf and tennis, and the vicarious, inartistic pleasures of the modern world. The gardens, as always in Holland, are full of flowers. The avenues, we cannot call them streets, are alive with bicycles. We overtake a young girl in an unfamiliar costume, but like that of a milkmaid in a fairy story; and looking

19 Veere

back we can only note her lace cap and roll of hair upon the forehead, the curious chintz yokes upon her shoulders, which invoked
the milkmaid, and that this country maiden with the fresh colouring and fair hair is wearing spectacles.

She has come on her bicycle, need we say, from Spakenburg,
which is but a half-hour's ride away. Much nearer than that in a
car; and now, twisting in and out among the hotels and villas, we
try to find the road and lose it, but pick it up again behind some
houses. A country road that bends and curves and cares for nothing
but its own line of pleasure; that comes to a canal and crosses it,
runs along for some distance and doubles back again; that halts,
as though with the whole day to waste, while a bridge is lifted
to let a barge float by. And now the tall trees are left behind and
all memory of tennis courts and summer villas. The green dairy-
land begins, like a prairie in little, with flocks of geese and herds
of black and white Frisian cattle. A church tower, no higher than
a fingernail, lies out in the nursery immensity. For it is that of a
nursery wallpaper, though we know that it will take no more than
a few moments to cross from end to end, but the road curves re-
solutely away from the church tower, faces it, swings past it, and
points away again. The summer afternoon, like that slow barge, is
floating by. A pair of bicycles and two milkmaids pass us slowly, as
in a dream, and as though they had their whole youth to share with
the milkpails and the fishing nets. For we are aware that Spakenburg, really, is a little fishing harbour; that there are twin towns or
villages, Bunschoten and Spakenburg, one inland and the other
near the sea, just as we find, now, that there are two church towers,
one behind the other, and that we can see the low, one-storeyed
houses.

Bunschoten, it is to be inferred, is the village of the milkmaids;
Spakenburg that of the fishergirls. The one is in the meadows; the
other down upon the Zuyder Zee; but the two villages merge into
one another. They are nothing but one long village street. The
houses do not even have the green shutters of Staphorst; nor do
they stand apart and separate like the houses of those peasant
proprietors. They lie in long brick rows, and the street is full of

children. What is enchanting about the little girls is that they wear black bonnets tied beneath their chins. According to information, they wear these bonnets until they are 12 years old but, probably owing to war conditions, there seemed to be children a little older than that still wearing them, perhaps up to 14 or 15, bonnets of black sateen with edging or trimming of sham ostrich feathers framing their faces, short sleeves, and long skirts that nearly touch the ground. And it appears that upon Sundays they have a brooch of gold or silver on one side of their bonnets.

They all wear the bonnets, but the very small children have cotton caps, flowered cotton dresses, and chequered aprons, while their tight-fitting bodices and puffed sleeves make them to be like children, if they could be Dutch children and the sons and daughters, at that, of Dutch fishermen, in portraits by Bronzino, for that, exactly, and their fair hair, is of his date and period. This must be a costume that has come down unaltered from the sixteenth century. The babes-in-arms wear a cap, a blue and white patterned handkerchief draped over that, the puffed sleeves, and if we are to believe the authors of *The National Costumes of Holland,* and we never found them wrong, we might see a babe in a frock of dark green sateen, with lighter green foliage sprigged with blue and red blossoms; or, upon a feast day, black sateen of fine quality stencilled with gay colours.

Bunschoten, itself, is nothing. There is no other interest but the dresses and the exceptional good looks of the children, which makes of these two villages some of the happiest places in all Holland. For, by now, we are in Spakenburg where the street widens and has a creek or river running down the middle of it and a road on either side. At the end there is the harbour, some say three harbours, where the boats of the herring fleet lie safe in shelter. The herring fishing begins in October and lasts till March, and in summer they drag for flounders, eels, and sprats. We did not see the silver herrings flapping on their lines hung upon poles in the open, but there were eels in plenty, writhing, Medusa-like, indeed as though they were the snake locks of the goddess shorn off and heaped in wooden bales and barrels. The houses of the fishermen have three rooms apiece. They are fishermen's houses, to be known as such immediately by lovers of the old houses of Whitby and of Robin Hood's Bay, not because of those red roofs, but because of the sheds built out at the back for the smoking and curing of the catch. But at Spakenburg, when you look in the direction of the sea there is no sign of it, and nothing could be more different from the tidal rocks and huge cliffs of the North Riding. This is the inland sea, or Zuyder Zee; the herrings are the despised and cheap sort, the *panharing*, and hence the town is poor and unspoilt for that reason.

Those sheds behind the houses are one of the fascinations of Spakenburg, and so are the pairs of wooden clogs upon the doorsteps, a sight common to most of Holland but, somehow, exceedingly appropriate to this bucolic fishing place. You can wander round behind the houses and look on gardens high with hollyhocks, with perhaps a beehive or two, and on one of the green banks you may, as we did, surprise two young women who sat with their backs to us against a low brick wall, knitting and gossiping who, when they turned round, hearing our voices, were embarrassingly good looking, and with whom, on appearance, and had it been possible in point of language, it would have been a civilized pleasure to sit talking through the summer afternoon. For the women of Spakenburg are as handsome as the Frisians, but without that northern colouring and not having that excessively fair hair, and in an hour or two we could have learned much of this little town and its inhabitants and, perhaps, been able to discover why it is that Spakenburg, of all such little centres of local ways and costumes in Holland is, today, the most attractive and most pleasant. You have the feeling that it would be no penance to 'marry into' Bunschoten or Spakenburg, where it would be unthinkable for a stranger to condemn herself or himself to living at Staphorst, or to life imprisonment upon the isle of Marken. Perhaps Volendam with its robust fishwives and fishermen is no unpleasant alternative to the amateur who is a Catholic. The Spakenburgers are Calvinists, but not dour and unforgiving as the Staphorsters, and on that summer afternoon there was no top-hatted shadow of the 'dominie' to throw a gloom along the sunlit brick paved street. It is not here, but at Hoogeveen, in Drenthe, that the Protestants are summoned to church according to ancient custom by beat of drums three times on Sundays, a drum, we add, that is painted red, blue, and white, the colours of Holland, and that is kept at other times, as though it is the weapon of punishment wielded by the headmaster, in the vestry, behind the pulpit.

Here and now, perhaps the moment has come to discuss in a single paragraph the double mystery of the costume communities in Holland. In the first place, except for a plate or two in Maaskamp, it is of no use to consult the costume books of last century, the period of such publications, for in no instance do they deal fairly with their subject. The works consulted give illustrations of the costume, both of Marken and of Volendam, that bear no relation whatever to the costume as it is worn today. Not only that, but the costumes are notably mid-nineteenth century at a time when we know, on the contrary, that they were more extraordinary by far than they are now. This, for instance, when the white mitre caps of Marken, which more nearly resembled the *kloboúk* of a Greek or Russian bishop, and the *zevenkleurige rokken* or seven-coloured skirts of Volendam, were of universal wear. But the dresses of Marken and Volendam in the books in question look dull and not worth seeing. Writers seem to have been quicker than painters in grasping how queer and peculiar the dresses were. Then, again, if we are to credit the writers, the inhabitants of Marken were remarkable for beauty. Havard speaks of 'rosy cheeks, fair hair, and, above all, very white teeth'. In his time they were 'handsome country girls', and he says that 'nothing is more gay than the young girls in their rose-coloured garments in the green meadows, with their ringlets floating in the air'. In his day, three generations ago, there were few signs of idiocy and of the physical penalties of too much inbreeding. Those have increased fatally and rapidly since his time, until it might be said, ungallantly, and in apprehension of a next landing on that siren quay, near to the painted cabins, that the greater part of the female population of Marken borders on imbecility, and is more than a little eccentric in its mode of welcome to visitors disembarking in the fish-laden breezes. There would seem to be communities that are doomed through continual intermarrying; some that are in a healthy condition through fresh blood; and others that are now in the pristine state of Marken, Urk, or Staphorst, as those were 100 years ago. Such are Spakenburg, and when we reach them, Walcheren, and the other isles of Zeeland. Of all the Dutch peasant costumes that of Spakenburg is by far the prettiest. Not only of the children, but of the grown young girls and women. Its particular beauty consists in that yoke of glazed and starched chintz across the shoulders, and it will be remembered that it was this that we noticed in the 'milkmaid' of Spakenburg, whom we saw riding her bicycle among the summer villas of Baarn, wearing spectacles. Not often can it be said of the Dutch costumes that their aim is physical attraction, so that it was a pleasurable feeling to be at large in a fishing village full of pretty milkmaids. In a land of which the cleanliness has passed into a proverb we can only suggest that the women of Spakenburg must have the highest laundry bills in Holland. Their washing, of course, is done in their own homes, and nothing could match the starching and laundering of their white lace caps. They have a tight roll of hair upon their foreheads, an innovation of fashion it seems, that has developed in the last few years, for, formerly, their hair was not visible, but now an arch of it quite frames their faces. A feature of the Spakenburg costume is the scarf or fichu, of scarlet, or crimson and white checked cotton, wrapped like a muffler round their necks, pinned down their fronts and crossed diagonally down their backs, the centre piece, as it were, of the costume, between the shoulder yokes. They wear blue aprons over skirts of dark blue, home-woven wool, called *zelferij,* while the yokes to their dresses and their half-sleeves, also, are of red and white checked Frisian cotton.

White lace caps; blue skirts and aprons; red and white checked mufflers; half-sleeves, yokes in different shades of scarlet or crimson to their dresses; and there remain those images of the milk pails from the yokes upon their shoulders. This most beautiful invention in the realm of peasant costume consists of a length of glazed, starched chintz doubled over to form a cuff, it could be called, for each shoulder. Scientifically described, it is nothing but an eccentric development of the *kraplap* for a particular purpose, the carrying of a pair of milk pails on a wooden yoke. The fresh laundering of these shoulder ornaments is the peculiar delight of the Spakenburg costume; but they project an inch or two at either side, their design is of green leaves and red or blue flowers upon a ground of white, often with a dotted background which gives richness. The variety of flowered patterns seems endless, and they are varied by the purple and white, or darker chintz yokes of the women who are in mourning.

These lovely inventions, for what else are we to call them, they are not shoulder pads, are worn even by the younger girls, those who wear the black ostrich feather bonnets, and who run so noisily along the street in their long blue skirts and wooden clogs. There are some beautiful chintz patterns worn among them; and for sleeves and bodices an astonishing variety of red checked cottons, a lesson in what effects can be achieved by mere differences in thickness of line and different weight of squaring. But, returning to the chintz yokes upon their shoulders, we conceive of them in image, as a kind of armour, for they resemble the mediaeval shoulder plates. Walking in twos and threes, with the peculiar gait conditioned by their long skirts and wooden clogs, generally with their knitting in their hands, the young women of Spakenburg belong to no date or period but exist in a world of their own, of which the frontiers are a half-day's ride upon a bicycle, the little world of the meadows and the fishing nets. The insides of their milk pails are often painted blue for mere ornament and beauty, and it can be in no other spirit that they evolved this costume. It is the same instinct that is at work among the birds of paradise; that evolved their metallic gorgets, their pectoral shields, and coloured streamers. At a cost of a few pence for a piece of glazed chintz, the costume of Spakenburg was transformed, when or how we know not, into a thing of beauty.

8. Dutch Gardens

Upon the authority of Horace Walpole, and other iconoclasts and lovers of the English landscape garden, it is assumed that it was 'Dutch William' who brought the taste for topiary, clipped hedges, green 'rooms', and the formal conceits of the Dutch garden to England, and not a little surprising, therefore, to be told by Dutchmen that, in Holland, this artificial style is laid at our doors and called an English garden. Such a bandying of names and nationalities, more often accorded to the pox and other maladies that it is impolite to mention, implies something of the old dislike for the drilled garden, a phrase of our own coining, having in mind that notorious garden of William of Orange which copied the plan – was it of a siege or a mere battle? – but it was complete with redoubts and batteries and companies of grenadiers, all in topiary, and growing taller with the years. The plaything of a martinet in a periwig, a great soldier who only relaxed in male company and preferred the statues of Mars and his minions to that of Venus, but no more need be said of this extreme and stilted specimen of a Dutch garden. We can visit, later, what instances of the Dutch style are to be found in England, of necessity, because there is so little left in Holland, its land of origin. Our concern, for the moment, is principle rather than example; and we begin with the formal features that the Dutch admired in flowers.

The Dutch gardeners are still, as they always have been, great florists. But taste has moved away and left us with only the 'parrot' tulips out of all the striped and marbled textures that they loved.

We lack space for an account of the tulip mania, except to say that speculation in tulip bulbs does not seem sillier, intrinsically, than any other form of gambling in a non-existent commodity, and we only mention the single bulb of 'Semper Augustus', a crimson and white 'flamed' tulip, that was bought for 13,000 florins in 1609. 'Semper Augustus', the most famous of Dutch tulips, survives, on paper, in a drawing; and how many more beautiful tulips there are, with lost names, in Dutch and Flemish paintings! The tulip mania was followed in the eighteenth century by a craze for hyacinths, especially the double ones. The plate of double hyacinths in Curtis's *The Beauties of Flora* is almost the only surviving relic of this fever. But I have by me a Catalogue of Foreign Flower Roots imported by a nurseryman of Leamington, 'near Warwick', as late as 1825, which lists no fewer than 38 double blues, 32 double reds, 46 double whites, and a mere eight double yellows. They have all Dutch or French names that are a delight in themselves.

The Dutch love for flowers is, of course, conditioned by what is lacking in the landscape. Italian gardens, we need only say, were never famous for their flowers. The shade of a terrace, a cypress, and a fountain, such is an Italian garden in its most simple terms; and in a land of vines and lemons they did not want the flaunting colours of a tulip. That, and the other florists' flowers, are for grey skies; but, also, we like to imagine, in symbol of the Dutch Eastern trade and of what their galleons had brought back to them from both Indies. The tulip mania and the cult of the Turkish ranunculus are connected with the Oriental influence in so many of the costumes in the Dutch fishing villages; but, also, with the imaginative embellishment of their atlases and sea charts, which is one of the most wonderful of the minor arts of Holland during the golden age. Forms, we can only call these, of escapism, but in a subjective, not objective sense, for their purpose was not to escape in their own fancy into distant lands, but to bring those far-off countries back into their own homes. Hence, the flowered cotton and the marbled petal. Hence, also, the painted 'shell' sledges, and the reindeer and volcanoes that we find upon their maps. But, above all, the silken Orient of the tulip bed recalling the Mogul or the Grand Turk and their turbaned court.

So much for the flowers. Now for the gardens. The long terraces of Caprarola or Villa d'Este were not for the Dutch landscape. In that land of low horizons the rule of beauty was to enclose the foreground, and the formal avenues of Le Nôtre became clipped hedges, an innovation which exactly suited both the Dutch genius and the proportions of the scene. From the middle of the seventeenth century the comfortable circumstances of Dutch merchants and burghers, not excepting the Dutch noble families in their country houses, enabled a multitude of small gardens to be made. Such are the *Buitenplaatsen,* the country seats and pleasure gardens and pavilions at the water's edge. One old author writes that 'frequently on entering a Dutch town, the traveller passes through a whole street of such gazebos', and he mentions the inscription 'De vleesch potten van Egypte', written above the entrance to one of the tea gardens of Rotterdam. Only by omission through ignorance did we not enquire at Baarn, upon the way to Spakenburg for the handsome Chinese villas called, respectively, 'Pekin' and 'Canton'. But, metaphorically, those are upon the road to Broek-in-Waterland.

The more serious Dutch gardens, before they descended to absurdity, were as characteristic of Holland, we like to think, as the house of a retired sea captain by the harbour side. That is to say, they set out at every turn of view to be reminded of their natural setting. Dutchmen insisted that their houses should be built up out of the water, or at the water's edge. From Middachten, downwards, they rise wherever possible from the middle of a moat. We find there are instances where the moat is hexagonal, or diamond-shaped, and therefore entirely artificial, and there can be no doubt that the Dutch liked the sensation of having to cross a bridge in order to go from the house to the stables and the gardens. They did not feel at home unless there were waters to remind them of their canals. A clipped tree was as natural to their tastes as, to an Italian gardener, an orange or lemon tree in a terracotta pot. The conceits of tree clipping were brought to a higher degree of art than in any other country, just as the Dutch parterres, in old prints, are more thickly carpeted than any others. They had a particular love, too, for pleached walks, and their gardens were divided into as many green 'rooms' or cabinets as they could contrive. Fountains were hardly practicable in Dutch gardens for it was a matter of difficulty to get the pressure. But the moats or canals are nearly always, as may be imagined, enlivened with a pair of swans, vast flocks of which birds, according to old report, frequented 'the pure, sweet waters of the Waterland'.

A delightful feature of a recent visit to Holland in April 1973 was the opportunity to revisit Zeist where the château of William of Orange has been reconstituted as to its interior, the beautiful red brick of the outside freed of its plaster, and the formal parterres and avenues will in time be restored. The park lay-out had been upon a huge scale, the principal avenue or axis being three miles long.

But the writer, not for the first time, is left wondering what he can have been thinking of when he mentions the colony of Hernutes or Moravians (see p. 11, 126) 'still to be seen at Zeist, near Utrecht, in two rows of neat cottages, and a plain conventicle'. For the Moravian colony in question is established in two splendid, three- or four-floored brick buildings to either side of the approach to the château, built it would seem some years later when the château was unlived in. The 'two rows of neat cottages' are in fact of Place Vendôme, Place des Vosges, Lansdowne Crescent quality and make a glorious relic of the sensible, neat past.

The Royal Château of Het Loo is not far from Zeist in this beautiful wooded part of Holland, which to many Dutch people is their favourite part of the Kingdom. Here, indeed, it was Daniel Marot who was at work for his master who was, also, our King William III; and the palace has only a certain severity about its exterior and perhaps something a little different in the surrounding woods to make it not quite like a large old country house in England. The knowledge that there are wild boar in the woods for one thing, and the sense that it is modest and sensible in size. The work of restoration at Het Loo under the able hands that have brought the dead château of Zeist to life again – not least the removal of its stucco casing to reveal the beautiful brick beneath, and perhaps eventually the renewal of its parterres and orchards – will make of it a fitting monument to the golden age of The Netherlands and the Soldier King.

But the best-preserved garden of its kind in Holland must be that of Rosendaal, again near Arnhem, where once more the name of Daniel Marot is invoked. From him, or his associate pupils and designers, date a 'tea-pavilion' and a 'scallop' gallery, sensibly so called, with fountain niches and garden benches made bright with shells and corals, white marble dolphins appropriately *en poste* on pedestals at top of the cascade, and huge roses formed of pink and yellow shells in tribute to the name of the house. Another curious feature must be the two eagles, 'made of coral and looking rather like parrots', above the garden seats in the 'scallop gallery'. The Arnhem family, original owners of Rosendaal, had been friends of William III, who hunted here, and stayed in a lodge by the ubiquitous Marot on a hill near by. Queen Mary, wife of 'Dutch William', is reported as giving the lady of Rosendaal 'a garden cabinet full of Delft Ware'. Can this have been to ornament the tea pavilion? What might be regarded as the 'oddities' of Rosendaal and of the Dutch taste in gardening, is illustrated in the article from which this is quoted, with reference 'to the use of box, yew, and embroideries decorated with stones, glass and beads instead of flowering plants'. And this is carried further in a footnote stating that 'gardens containing ornaments filled with beads along the Zaan rivers were to be seen until the late nineteenth century in the region known as the Zaansteek, the inhabitants of which were Mennonites of conservative disposition. Merchants trading with Africa and the Indies used large quantities of beads, made of stone or glass and marbles, for purposes of barter or as currency in their dealing with native races'.*

* Quoted from an article *Country Houses in the Northern Netherlands, the way of life of a Calvinistic patriciate*, by H. W. M. van der Wicjk, in *Apollo* for November 1972.

Such will have been the 'mini-gardens' nearer Amsterdam, all swept away now. But for knowledge of what is lost that was upon a larger scale, we would refer the reader to the coloured plates, described below, that are contained in a set of volumes in the British Museum.

In default of surviving examples, the lover of Dutch gardens must be content with old accounts, or prints. For, so far as I know, there is not one existing specimen of an old Dutch garden. The formal park of Het Loo still has its avenues, but no parterres; while Rozendaal, near Arnhem, has, or had, a beautiful garden, though inclining to the landscape taste with classical temples and pavilions, but only the vestiges of what is implied in a Dutch garden. In so many places there are still the country houses, but without the gardens, which were swept away during the landscape craze. The old part of The Hague, it is true, still preserves with its malls and plantations on the Lange Voorhout the aspect of an early eighteenth-century town, and as much could be said of the three principal canals of Amsterdam with their patrician houses fronted by long lines of elms. But these are not gardens, and for existing Dutch gardens we shall have to go to England.

Our information comes mainly from a series of 11 huge volumes that have found their way into the Map Room of the British Museum, and that require a considerable degree of physical strength to handle. It is a collection composed of maps of Dutch towns, but among them, and for no particular reason, there are handcoloured views of gardens, the work, evidently, of a professional colourist, for they are most beautiful in execution, and heightened with gold in certain instances. Many sets of engravings, bound in with the volumes, are the work of Daniel Stoopendael, beginning for our present purposes with a series that depict the gardens of Klingendal, belonging to the de Brienen family, in the wood outside The Hague. One of the plates is of particular interest, for it shows the Dutch fashion of bedding out their florists' flowers, fringing, as it were, the embroidered parterres and nodding their heads above the clipped box and coloured pebbles. We move on into more volumes and come to gardens, Vriemond, Swanenborgh,

Vredenborgh, of which it is to be feared there are no traces left. Heemstede, near Utrecht, was a house that stood in a most elaborate polygon of a moat. And so we arrive, still examining the prints of Daniel Stoopendael, at *De Zegepraadlende Vecht*, translated, more picturesquely, as *La Triomphante Rivière de Vecht*, where, for it is worth the delay, we propose to halt awhile.

Or, better still, we will float along that lazy current, for this waterway, like the Brenta, is one of the forgotten rivers of civilization, so much so that I have to confess to never having heard of it myself until the summer in question (1947). The Vecht is the river flowing from Utrecht nearly to Amsterdam, for it debouches into the Zuyder Zee at Muiden; but during the eighteenth century it was the chief passage leading from Holland and England, we might say, into Europe, and throughout the 20 miles of its length it was lined on both sides with villas and gardens, belonging to the nobles and rich burghers of Amsterdam and Utrecht. To the Dutchmen it was equivalent to owning a house along the Champs Elysées, for up or down this river passed, at some time or other, everyone of consequence in Europe. The Vecht, therefore, was one of the glories of Holland, and they were as proud of this water corridor, flowing into their midst, as were the Venetians of the Brenta. Its glories were engraved by artists and extolled by poets. Monarchs, like our George II on the way to and from his Hanoverian dominions, were borne luxuriously up or down its stream, and so were many lesser persons of more lasting interest.

The vehicle was nothing other than a gilded barge, which floated down the current, but had to be drawn laboriously up the stream by horses, or in some of the engravings, by old women. Either way, up or down, this must have been a delightful journey; villas and gardens, as we have said, lined both the banks. I have before me upon my table another, an easier and more accessible, later edition of the same prints in a single volume, poems, engravings and all, but uncoloured, *De Vechtstroom van Utrecht tot Muiden* of 1790, soon after which date the Vecht lost its importance as a channel of communication and, one by one, its lovely gardens were destroy-

ed and swept away. The elephant folios of the Map Room, so re-
warding but wearying to handle, are two generations earlier; they
may date from 1730 when *La Triomphante Rivière* was in clipped
and planted glory, and the day's journey up or down the sluggish
stream must have been indeed a beautiful experience. With this
smaller book in hand let us embark, therefore, upon the waiting
barge. The only question is, shall we go up or down the Vecht, but
we are given our answer in the title and choose the falling stream,
from Utrecht to Muiden.

The beauty of this book, as of the coloured views, lies in the
contrast between the placid Dutch villages, unchanged in ages,
with their steep-roofed houses and bridges over the Vecht, and
the laughing gardens, topiary and parterre, albeit of a well-trained,
not a natural, laugh. A little way out of Utrecht, on the left bank
of the stream, we come to Sy-Baalen, where, at a wooden quay,
we climb out among the swans. The garden lies behind a plain
front, and has a basin of water elaborately dug with rounded edges
and set round with bay trees in their tubs. A screen of green
arches, box or yew, with busts on pedestals, is growing, though
we can hardly use that term of such a theatre scene, immediately
before the house. Its arches, exactly like scenery, spring from the
wall at either end, and they are echoed or repeated by more green
arches beyond the basin, with a centre view and conventional side
entrances cut into the green. This house, it is interesting to note,
when we remember the old interiors of Amsterdam, is described
as having a splendid room with paintings by Gerald Hoedt (1648–
1733), who was much in demand in that city and at The Hague
for his painted decorations.

We float on, lazily, past Zuylen, which is like a village forgotten
in a dream, and come to Maarsen, a delightful spot, still with one
or two gazebos at the water's edge, 'avec de riants environs' as it is
described, even now, and where the very hotels are called 'Con-
cordia' and 'De Harmonie'. The next villa we come to, Doomburg
(we speak in the present tense as though it is 1730, a happier year
than now), is the property of, or we will have it in Dutch, 'de
Plaats van Mejuffr. de Weduwe van de Hr. Will. Van Son,

Domheer van oud Münster', which means that it belongs to the widow of the Secular Canon of old Münster, and it is a pretty little place with a nice trim parterre, gardeners with rakes and wheelbarrows, and a few green obelisks. We pass on again, by Elsenburg, where the Vecht is on the curve, where there are persons fishing, and a young lady and gentleman are seated on a bench before a fine iron gate; past Soetendael, belonging to Mr Isaac Simons, a member, it must be, of the Sephardic colony; past a ferry with two banks of seats opposite one another like the old 'Lonsdale' in which, as a child staying with my grandmother, I was taken twice to church on Sundays; past the *Plaats* of Mr David Mendes de Silva, another of the rich Portuguese Sephardim; and we tie up at Hoogevecht. Here, too, is another ferry with ladies and gentlemen sitting ready for the crossing; the garden is on a big scale with green obelisks and elaborate parterres, a basin of water with statues on green mounds at its angles, but, somehow, I do not much like Hoogevecht. I prefer Otterspoor, which is but 100 yards away. But it is midday. A barge comes by with a clinking of glasses and a noise of revelling, and we decide to stop for luncheon.

Afterwards we walk in the gardens of Otterspoor, past the fish ponds, and down the long canal, with green 'rooms' or 'cabinets' to either side; and then embark again, casting off among a family of swans and coming almost immediately to Gansenhof, the property of a rich lawyer of Amsterdam, where we find more swans floating in front of what is nothing other than a garden theatre. There is a low clipped hedge with green obelisks at intervals, and a dip in it not to impede the view of actors or dancers, water where the orchestra should be, two trim bridges at either side like flights of steps into the wings, bay trees and more green obelisks for footlights, and solid green scenery, a 'built' scene of beech or hornbeam, set up like a pair of screens with statues and busts on pedestals, and a long perspective entrance in the middle. Nyenroode, a bigger, older house, comes next, with a drawbridge of its own and a nest of storks upon the roof; and then a pretty little house with nothing but a green hedge in front of it along the tow path, and a line of bay trees and green obelisks. The village of

Breukelen appears in the near distance (Breukelen being the derivative of New York's Brooklyn), and just short of it there is the house and garden of Mijnheer Theodoor Boendermaker, in our view the most agreeable of all the villas along the Vecht.

It announces itself by a splendid, high temple of latticework perched upon a mound, and by the sight of various green tunnels, latticed arches, and the backs of what must be fountains or grottoes, enclosed, as it were, in boxes of masonry. Here we are interrupted by a boat that comes past with a bellying sail, scattering the cygnets, but we come up again to the poplars and green hedges and will halt for a moment. It is a small house, with a façade of but five windows, little pavilions to either side, and a high, curving hornbeam hedge joining the house to the river by means of that pair of grottoes with their fronts of latticework and plain, flat backs. Little the house may be, but we wish it were possible to see inside it, for it has two rooms painted by Isaac Moucheron, 'Ordonnance' (1670–1744). The garden, which has parterres as richly embroidered as a beau's goldlaced waistcoat, is set about with green yew pyramids and statues on high pedestals; there is a low green wall with a waved top to it, cut in 'ups' and 'downs' at the Vecht's edge, by the footlights, and a low railing has been built out on a projecting platform flanked by a pair of urns, as though this is the bandstand for the orchestra. But the garden continues behind the house; there is a big basin of water with obelisks that reflect themselves, a high green gazebo at the far end, the lattice-work temples at either side on the mounds, and in the middle an affair of pillars and architraves like a *gloriette*, in the taste of the theatre, again, for it stands on a green rampart that suggests another stage.

And, re-embarking, we float down the waterfront of a ghostly Brooklyn thinking, it may be, of Manhattan and Haarlem and hearing a discordant music on the breeze. Soon we are brought back into the living present by a boy riding a horse that pulls a barge upstream and by meeting a party of gentlemen, pistols in holsters, who are riding out from Amsterdam. Queekhoven is the next villa, with a landing stage; and according to our old guide,

20 *Delft in spring*

rather surprisingly, it is 'L'Ecole de pension de Mons. Pierre Mannoury', or, in fact, a boarding school. It has clipped hedges in front; we hear the voice of the pedagogue from an open window, and coming round behind, down a garden alley, we find ourselves in a delightful garden scene, or rather, turning, we look back through the gate and are in an open space where some half-dozen of the pupils are playing bowls in the dust. We are in front of a canal with swans, and the sides of the bridge have been converted into wide, curving benches where you may sit and look round at the high clipped hedge behind you, and along its terrace by the water with trees and green pyramids, and a pair of gardeners at work upon the hornbeam. A parent with an important child, dressed like its father with tricorne and walking stick, strides out to luncheon, and more parents and grandparents make in our direction. Now we return slowly down that green mall; other barges come past, there are ferries, and horsemen and small two-wheeled carriages with hoods, drawn at a trot along the path or *sandpad*.

Groenevecht, of the charming name, need not long delay us. It has a little bridge, which can be drawn up so that we may float to it down its own canal; and at the back nothing much but green arches, two storeys high like wings to the house, with doors and windows cut in them; a flower garden with yew obelisks at the corners, standing upon bases cut correctly according to the rules of architecture; and gardeners with wheelbarrows or trimming hedges. A warning bugle rings out from a pleasure barge as we float in front of a villa with a gazebo built out into the water. And another villa, within 100 yards, has a trellised temple at either end of its terrace, a padlocked boathouse, and a multitude of hand-fed swans. The Vecht bends opposite the 'Maison de Plaisance' of Sr. Benjamin Teixeira, a wealthy and, of course, bearded member of the Sephardim; and we see beyond it, Overholland and its high trees, a great banqueting temple on a raised plinth, by the water, from which to watch the barges floating up and down; the next villa with low clipped hedge, gazebo, and boathouse below and lanterned landing stage; and Rupelmonde with its long

21 *The Mauritshuis, The Hague*

pleached walk or green arcade along the water. Here, someone is fishing with a dragnet. At another curve of the river we come to Ouderhoek, which has a garden sporting the tallest green obelisks of all and a pavilion visited three times by 'Sa Majesté Czarienne' in 1717, the European tours of Peter the Great being attended with as much sycophancy as those of his political equivalents in their tours of the Russian satellite states of to-day. This garden, and it is a pleasure to be back in it after the mere utterance of a name, has green compartments like the segments of a jigsaw puzzle, and a fish pond or *vivier de carpes* with pleached alleys round it, cut like a green cloister. The house, and we must regret not to have seen it, has a painted room by Philip Tideman (1657–1705).

In another garden, from which we see a passing sail above a clipped hedge, there is a pretty parterre, much trimming of hornbeam, and another of the bridges that are really banks of seats. Nieuwerhoek, a villa that is nothing remarkable in itself, has a charming garden behind it, parterres, rows of green obelisks, and a swan pond with a pavilion on a causeway in the middle. There is an arch under this pavilion so that you may see through it, over a balcony, to the pond beyond, and a painted swan with a golden collar perches on its pedestal at the apex of the roof. An old house, nearly a castle, next appears with new additions, and under its terraced walk we watch the swans floating among the reflections of the bay trees. What a pleasant stretch of river! The tow path is planted with a row of poplars, there are gazebos or summer houses in the distance, and a great white sail against the whiter, summer clouds. Here the Vecht widens into a river basin, there are sails on smaller boats scudding across the pool, and the church of Loenen fills the foreground as though this is the river's end. The family have arrived and are just driving down the avenue in their four-horsed coach, for there is a house here belonging, not to a banker or lawyer of Amsterdam, but to the local landowner; not a large house, it is four-square, with a cupola, and a garden of alleys and green cabinets. Next door is another country house with a very pretty garden of embroidered parterres, and what we can only call, having regard to their theatre air, green wings or screens leading to an ornamental pool of water.

A little farther, and opposite to a pair of swans fighting and to some men fishing from a wooden jetty, we come to Oostervecht, the *Lustplaats* of Heer Isaac Simkinson, another Jew from Portugal, we conjecture; and to a house hidden in trees, to boats using dragnets, and to a large wooden causeway into the bulrushes; followed by an old castlet with turrets, standing in a moat and approached by a drawbridge, the property of Heer Wellard Godard van Tuyll van Serooskerken, a famous name in Holland. We are nearing Muiden; there are boats with flat decks covered with merchandise and a view of many windmills. And we come to Petersburg, the most magnificent of the Vecht villas, belonging to a Dutchman who is Russian Consul or Resident in Amsterdam, a village that is approached by a landing stage under a species of triumphal arch. The garden, of which there are no fewer than 11 engravings in our guide, lies behind the house. It consists of a carp pond or *vivier* with statue of Neptune, trident in hand, and from the back of the house project line after line of the green wings or screens, nearly as high as the building itself. There is a *grande allée* where the giant Czar walked often, taller than the yew pyramids, triton fountains and other flashing waters, an orangery, a Russian bath, a string orchestra playing under the hornbeams, more green alleys with turf carpets, a circular swan pool, the *dernier bassin* and *dernier cabinet,* the *berceau* or long pleached walk, a pavilion on a mound or *petite montagne* where 'leurs majestés Czariennes' found much pleasure and looked out upon the windmills and distant steeples; and passing a fortress, dull as are fortresses anywhere, in any clime, we come to Driemond, the last of the Vecht villas, eight engravings of it, a most delightful house of red brick with six flat Corinthian stone pilasters to the waterfront, swags under the windows, a high 'hipped' roof with a balustrade and cupolas, and a lovely little garden running down to the river, a garden with a simple parterre, and enclosed by high green screens. At the back, there is the usual pond with yew obelisks, a Neptune fountain at the stone edge, there are gardeners with long 'half-moons' or sickles trimming the gigantic hedges, a kitchen garden, a stables with an *oeil-de-boeuf* window cut into the hornbeam, a semicircular pond with a stone obelisk rising in the middle, and another piece of water with embroidered flower-beds behind it and a backing of green screens and arches. But there are no more villas and we emerge, past windmills beyond counting, in the port of Muiden.

Such is the Vecht in the 100 views or engravings, but of course there are other villas, like Marquette of the lovely wrought iron gates, that lie off the actual course of the Vecht, but within a mile or two, and along the old road from Amsterdam to Utrecht, and are, therefore, omitted from the old book. We have been looking at the villas of the Vecht in the book of black and white engravings, but in the sumptuous folios of the Map Room they appear in colour, in little handcoloured plates no bigger, sometimes, than vignettes, all of which are a delight to look at and examine; but there are particular instances, Boendermaker or Vriemond, that are small masterpieces of neat elegance and that give a lovely vision of this departed way of life. The red brick of the villas is rendered a rose-petal or grape-bloom blue, and there is exquisite pleasure in the green wings and arches, so that it is impossible to conceive of a profession other than gardener in these Elysian and trim scenes along the water. But there are the various series of engravings bound up with the folios, including many great double-page engravings, heightened with gold, and handcoloured to a standard of minute and sparkling brilliance not excelled even in that great theatrical collection of the Hofburg in Vienna which some of our readers may recall in the 12 volumes of *Monumenta Scenica*. Together with the smaller half-page miniatures these coloured engravings in the Map Room must form one of the most important documents of the art and history of the formal garden.

Still by Daniel Stoopendael, there are splendid plates of the gardens and château of Voorst, in the wooded country between Zutphen and the River Yssel, a house much destroyed or damaged in the war. The double-page engraving shows the front of the château, its railing and forecourt crowded with arrivals, and the parterres or carpets of the formal garden. Later, we are taken in detail into the green cabinets, for we are now in more ambitious settings than those of the villas along the Vecht. They were the property, as we know, chiefly of lawyers and rich merchants of Amsterdam, but here we are among the feudal landowners and nobles. These are not summer villas along a river; they are family châteaux in great parks. Voorst had a painted staircase by Daniel Marot, closely resembling that of Het Loo, and mentioned at its appropriate moment when we spoke of the great influence of this Huguenot craftsman and architect in Holland. He it was who brought Versailles to Holland, and we might almost say to Hampton Court.

Another fine and less crowded plate, interesting because it gives figures of Dutchmen in their baggy breeches among the huntsmen and retainers, depicts this same château of Voorst, the property of the Keppels, Earls of Albemarle.* The château, it will be seen, is modest in size, but delightful in the formal balance of its parts, following the typical William and Mary plan of a square block with side pavilions, a forecourt, a railing, and wrought iron gates. It is reminiscent of English houses, big and small, of the pattern of Nether Lypiatt in Gloucestershire, and only Dutch by reason of the baggy breeches of the peasants and by its material being brick, not stone, and of the thin Dutch bricks, at that, not those fired in the English clay kilns.

But a greater artist now appears in the Dutch gardens. This is the engraver Romeyn de Hooghe (1646–1708), nephew, some say, of the more famous painter, and best known for his book illustrations to the *Fables* of La Fontaine and to *Les Indes Orientales et Occidentales,* a most extraordinary work of the imagination, and one which was to have a lasting influence upon tapestry and

* Arnold Joost van Keppel, the favourite of William III, and his son William-Anne, both Knights of the Garter, the latter (christened as a future courtier, with an eye to alternatives, upon the modern principle of Safety First) a famous soldier, settled in England, and left a title which is still borne by his descendants.

lacquer designers and upon the painters and modellers of Meissen porcelain, upon all those, in short, who chose the Orient for subjects. In his other work, Romeyn de Hooghe, by whom we saw some indifferent frescoes in the Town Hall at Enkhuizen, was an engraver of historical and military scenes in a style derived from Callot. I was not previously aware of his engravings of Dutch gardens. A work which is not included in the collection of folios in the Map Room is devoted to the fountains and gardens of Het Loo. The best of the engravings is, perhaps, one in which we are shown an enclosed garden or 'cabinet' of topiary, the clipped yew trees taking the form of hooded porters' chairs in old fashioned entrance halls. The rest of the book is an affair of parterres and fountains.

But we return to the collection of folios in the Map Room, for Romeyn de Hooghe's garden engravings must be seen in colour. There are other plates of Het Loo by his hand; and a series depicting Soestdijk and another of William III's Dutch hunting châteaux. In one of these, I write from memory, we have some wonderful four-wheeled coaches, drawn up in a castle courtyard, and a military scene with an escort of cavalry and with the foot guards presenting arms. In another, those distant times are brought nearer to us by the arrival of one of William III's baggage wagons with the Royal arms of Great Britain and Ireland (and the French lilies) painted on the back of its canvas hood. There is a scene, also, of the return of the hunting party to the courtyard of Het Loo, or that other of the castles. The dead stag is brought back in its tumbril; the hounds are on their *hardes*, six or eight upon a lead; there is a crowd of onlookers; and to the left, along the frozen canal, for there is a canal, of course, we see one of the 'swan' sledges bringing back the ladies from hunting,* we get the

---

* Compare, too, the hunting cart in the Rijksmuseum, with paintings by Aart Schouman (1710–92), a painter of The Hague who specialized in birds and animals, painted scenes from Ovid's *Metamorphoses* and, also, was an engraver upon crystal. His engraved glasses are the subject of a monograph by Wilfred Buckley (London: Methuen & Co., 1931). Monographs by the same writer deal with the engraved glasses by Frans Greenwood and D. Wolff.

smell, almost, of the gathering mists of evening, and have in our ears the haunting prelude to *Le Lac des Cygnes*.

Romeyn de Hooghe has to be seen, however, in his garden masterpiece, here present, handcoloured, in the folios. Although the garden it depicts is in Flanders, not Holland, being, in fact, 30 miles as the swan flies – an hour's flight? – why must it always be a crow? – from the French frontier, we feel tempted to include it, for the engraver Romeyn de Hooghe was a Dutchman, it is the only garden out of The Netherlands that is depicted by him, and in spite of its great size and scale, in comparison with the typically French Le Nôtre garden of Beloeil, near by, it represents the principles and precepts of the Dutch garden. This wonderful theme is the garden of the château d'Enghien, close to the town of that name, and lying south of Brussels. It must have been, truly, among the wonders of all Europe, and we return in imagination to its green glories, time and time again. The property had been an ancient possession of the houses of Luxemburg and Bourbon, hence the title of Duc d'Enghien, which remained in the family of Bourbon Condé, but the fief was sold by Henri iv to the Ducs d'Aremberg, who were sovereign princes of the Empire with great estates in many countries. The château was destroyed in the French Revolution, but traces of the old garden and the avenues remain.

The great folding plate of the gardens of Anghiana, as the name is Latinized, is as beautiful and difficult to follow as the tapestry of a plan of battle. The whole of the garden scene spreads out before us, attacked by Romeyn de Hooghe with a superb energy and dash. We are standing at an imaginary point whence we can see the entire garden, or, rather, it is as though we are approaching it at great speed in a low-flying aeroplane. The grand entrance is in the middle of an immense hornbeam hedge, the probable length of which we are able to conjecture from the hornbeam alleys of Beloeil, referred to in a later footnote. Down its whole length, this lateral road, leading along the hedge, is crowded with coaches and horsemen and persons of less consequence on foot, all bound for the great gardens. This concourse of figures, ant-like in dimensions, is rendered with the verve of Callot, and brilliantly coloured. Immediately in front of us, in sharp perspective, lead the slant hedges of the entrance alley, and Romeyn de Hooghe has imparted to the hornbeam ramparts the abrupt urgency of the entrance to a fortress. His excitement is communicated to ourselves, and in a rapture we look down the green corridor towards the extraordinary stockade or maze, a plantation of trees in regular segments like the fragments of a honeycomb – with a great fountain, more like a castle, in the middle – which crowns the horizon and is one of the features of this green architecture of an age of giants. It was a wooded fort of seven bastions that overlooked the shooting ranges. To both sides the huge scheme extends, and all the ingenuity of the Dutch or Flemish school of garden architects is here displayed and exemplified upon an heroic scale. To the left of the main axis there are wired enclosures for rare animals and an aviary for pheasants and exotic birds. Upon the other side there is a great basin or *pièce d'eau* with pleasure boats as large as galleons afloat upon it. In the distance we see the green colosseum, a Roman theatre in green ruins contrived of yew and hornbeam, and one of the wonders of Enghien. To balance it, there is upon the other side a lake with the so-called 'La Motte', an artificial island like a green redoubt or fortress, with a high-throwing fountain in the middle, a military caprice which is carried further, we now notice, in the green bastions shaped like spearheads or arrowheads which project from the great formal stockade or maze, of mysterious purpose, and that give to it a semblance of the toy fort of Naarden and the salients and circumvallations of Vauban and his school.

The more poetical beauties of Enghien are to be found, however, in the green cabinets which we now enter, passing under a gateway where the *trabants* or halberdiers are on guard, dressed in doublets and breeches that are the crimson counterpart to the Swiss Guard. Upon these green cabinets all the images and resources of the metaphysical garden of the late seventeenth century have been lavished, and we may wonder where to enter, for it consists of a pair of enclosed cabinets of two compartments each – would it be more simple to call it a long parallelogram hedged and

divided into four? – and we choose the approach by water, from
the other side, disembarking at a corridor of green arches, hedges
cut square at the top, with long windows clipped and contrived
in them as regular as the openings in a colonnade, a green passage
set down, and growing, at the landing stage, to lead into Elysium.
In the first cabinet there is a green temple; and before you enter
into the other, beyond it, a round space set about with clipped
hedges that are like high green screens or shutters, or like 'sides'
or 'drops' of the green theatre, and that can be carried round and
put in place again. To the images of mime or dance evoked by this
conceit, there succeed the clipped walls or hedges of the green
cabinets, which are trained over into long shaded walks or arbours
with arched windows cut into them at regular intervals, embra-
sures through which the gallants lean out talking to their ladies.
Along other of the green walls there are statues so contrived that
they appear to be leaning or reclining upon green shelves cut into
the hedges.*

The gardens of Enghien, of which there are but the ruins left,
but which in their prime must have compared in scale with the
great seventeenth-century gardens of Italy and France, form the
grandest examples ever created of the Dutch or Flemish school.†
They will have contained the choicest specimens of the Dutch
florists, and it is tempting to pursue their art and that of the

* Other features of the gardens at Enghien were the Mall, an alley
three hundred yards long, enclosed in high hedges, and with raised side
walks from which to watch the game. The Orangery, according to Loudon,
the English landscape gardener, contained one hundred and eight orange
trees in tubs, many of them two hundred years old, and presents from the
kings of Spain, with straight stems of six and eight feet and 'globular
heads, from which protruding shoots and blossoms are pinched off as soon
as they appear, for culinary and perfumery purposes.' In summer the
orange trees in their tubs were brought out and formed into an orange-
grove.

† Belœil, by contrary, is entirely a garden in the French style. The
grande pièce d'eau, as splendid as an inland sea, must be nearly half a mile in
breadth. The pleached hornbeam alleys extend for five kilometres, and in
layout this is a garden as splendid as Versailles. This great domain of the
de Ligne family has, however, little or no sculpture. It is not, apparently,
by Le Nôtre himself, but is a garden in his style and manner.

topiarist in England, to the clipped gardens of Chastleton or Levens Hall, or to that of Packington House, in the Forest of Arden, which is a representation, in yew, of the Sermon on the Mount. There is a complete fragment of a Dutch garden, a long straight canal with a gazebo at the end, no more than that, at Westbury-on-Severn in Gloucestershire, on the far or Welsh bank of the Severn; but this is a subject that could only be studied in entirety were there an exhibition held of those 'primitive' house and garden paintings often to be found in old houses, up and down England. Few old houses, indeed, are without them, and they have more of aesthetic value than is yet realized. A notable specimen hangs at Crichel in Dorset : while the mention in an old guide that 'the old house at Haigh Hall, near Wigan, in Lancashire, was celebrated for its quaint and formal Flemish gardens and groves, of which an interesting and curious picture, as they existed at the beginning of the eighteenth century, is still extant', but whets the appetite for more.

We are recalled from England to Holland, however, at the last moment before going to press, by the appearance in a London saleroom of a magnificently bound volume, 'contemporary Dutch morocco, tooled in gold with a pattern of a triumphal arch surmounted by a crown, supported by angels, shaped inlay of black morocco in centre, triple outer border of gold ornaments', etc. etc., which volume, consisting of four separate books of views, bound up as one, forms a complement to that superb coloured series in the Map Room. These engravings, published in Amsterdam, are by Abraham Rademaker (1675–1735), 'who was well acquainted with the rules of architecture, and whose first productions were painted in watercolours and were very highly finished', and we conclude our account of Dutch gardens with a quick survey of his pages. The first series bears the pretty title, *Miroir des Délices dans la belle saison d'Amsterdam, vers les villages d'Amstelveen, Slooten, et de la Chaussée,* and embarking with him on the canal, where laundry is being beaten on a wooden landing stage and there is a close view of many windmills, we find no cause to stop except to admire the high four-wheeled wagons,

drawn by four horses, or the smaller two-wheeled chariots, until
we come, by more windmills and past a cotton printing factory,
to the 'jardin de plaisance du Seigneur de Brueil', a most delightful and typical red brick building, a tall body with little balustraded wings and a pair of *oeil-de-boeuf* windows to each, a formal gate
with stone urns, square gazebos at the corners, yew pyramids, and
the inevitable green corridor or tunnel, to which succeed a
pair of views of Slooten and Amstelveen, Brueghel villages; one,
curiously, with a notice board and a high hooded wagon rolling
away from us down the middle of the village street, and the first
series ends.

The second, bearing the yet more engaging title, *La Hollande
en toute son Eclat et Beauté en trente vues,* opens with a milkmaid, yoke on shoulder, on a canal bank near a country house;
followed by another villa with a fine gate and an ornamented
landing stage, yew pyramids in the distance, and a complication
of pier and water that must delight the small boy walking there. A
villa, 'Weltevreden' ('Bien Content'), has a high Dutch mirror
back, a water pavilion with balcony at the corner, and hedges cut,
quaintly, like the backs of chairs. There follows a country house
entered through a gateway bearing the figure of a unicorn; and,
next, we find ourselves before an immensely tall building, reached
by steps, with long sash windows, and a pair of sails, with pennons,
showing above the wall. The grander house of Zwanenburg, with
a pair of bridged entrances and gate piers, with a waiting coach
and pair, comes next; and the much prettier villa of Sieur Jean
Veen, enclosed in hedges or high green shutters, a barge or
trekschuyt tying up, and a tall, brick summer house; a Brueghel,
thatched village with a gilded chariot, with red wheels, at the inn
door; and the village of Spaarndam curving with its high roofs
along a wooden wharf. The country houses grow grander in scale,
there are great coaches-and-four drawn up in front of them; we
come to a great house with a forecourt, and to another with a
pair of high stone obelisks, green 'scenes' and pyramids, and an
open railing set, specially, for us to see the garden. Another house
has what appears to be a wooden triumphal arch, with swags and

garlands, set up before it, and passing through more villages this series of engravings comes to an end.

We turn the page, and another series begins, still prefaced, like the others, with a long Dutch poem from the pen of G. Tyssens. The subject, this time, is *Holland's Arcadia* or the villas along the River Amstel, in 100 views, beginning with a *naumachia* or sham sea-fight in front of Amsterdam; and continuing, mysteriously, with a 'vue des prairies le long des jardins de l'éléphant'; to the backs of many summer houses, all in a row, with high-pitched roofs and haycocks in front, at the water's edge; to the bright yellow gateway to the country house of Mijnheer Dirk Slicher; past another wooden villa standing at a corner, with an immensely high, two-wheeled chariot, as awkward as a 'bonebreaker' or velocipede, drawn up outside it; past another cotton printing factory, and a small villa belonging to Mijnheer Jan Six, Burgomaster of the town of Amsterdam; by more villas, one of them the property of the euphoniously named Arnoldus Wittebol, to 'Solitudo', the house of Heer Reinders, but it has a balustrade and stands on a wharf with other buildings, and we arrive at a pair of country houses that have fine wrought iron gates with openwork gate piers of the richest workmanship. The country house, next after this, has a wooden gate, and bridge to it, with painted coats-of-arms; there are new forms of hooded chariots, with red wheels, and loaded haywains; and we are at the *bombé,* bombastic gateway to the villa of Heer Manuel Ximenes, Baron de Bellomonte, of the Sephardim; and thence, among its yew pyramids, to another garden that has a round gazebo shaped like a gasometer. The villa of Heer David de Pinto, one more of the Lusitanian Sephardim, has the most elaborate of the iron gateways; and passing the country house of the 'Directeur de la Compagnie des Indes Orientales', in Dutch, 'Bewindhebber der Oostindische Maatschappij', it is more pleasing still, we float by a square gazebo built out into the water, past more haywains, and the villa of Heer Bueno, to a delightful, crowded, and convivial part of the river bank, where are the houses of Heeren Schepper and Libarius, one of whom, already drinking with a friend, awaits us on a platform built out like a bandstand at the water's edge, under a trellised archway. Then come more villas, built close together, each with a summer house upon the water, and we reach the 'Maison de Plaisance de Madame de Gillon', with perhaps the most beautiful of the little gardens, a wooden landing stage with benches, a pair of tall piers, and a hedge trimmed elaborately with battlements and round windows in it, and the tall house behind with pillared frontispiece and side pavilions with pillared doorways. Little gardens, farther on, with plain wooden palings and but a row or two of yew obelisks, and now a multitude of blue-tiled roofs of houses and gazebos, farm wagons, high curricles, men on horseback riding along the tow path, men with dragnets, and slow barges with loose flapping sails; and we are at Abcoude, a village where we have been before not in person, in order to visit its chapel or mausoleum by Daniel Marot, ending our journey among a crowd of little pavilions set round with high hoops or arches, like May garlands, but they are tall hoops of yew or hornbeam; there are windmills and haycocks and we come in sight of Amsterdam.

Les Plus Agréables Vues du Rhynland, treating of villas and villages between Haarlem and Leyden, passes Rosendaal, which is the country home of Heer Gillis Jillis, and seeing nothing to which we are not accustomed but a pair of hornbeam walls with buttresses, we reach a plain house with pilasters and a high roof, but it is enclosed in the most perfect green theatre wings; and there is nothing more except an older house with yew hedges so tall that there is space in them for two rows of busts in niches, one above the other, until we come to Leyden. Views of Alkmaar, Delft, and Dordrecht form the conclusion of this great collection; but there is little of garden interest if we except the picturesquely named 'Bosquet des Anabaptistes' at Alkmaar, there are but the gardens of hospitals and almshouses, and we reach the back binding and are admiring, once again, the 'triumphal arch in gold tooling on red morocco, surmounted by a crown, supported by angels'. Its contents have given us the gardens and country houses on the outskirts of Amsterdam, and it is the complement to our voyage from

Utrecht down the River Vecht. What is lacking in our account
is some description of the Dutch country houses in the provinces of
Gelderland, in the neighbourhood of Arnhem and Apeldoorn,
round Deventer and Zutphen, of which the Bentinck châteaux
of Middachten and Amerongen may be the principal, but there
are many more. This is the region of the Dutch country houses
belonging to the old aristocracy of The Netherlands. Their wealth
in old furniture and silver and in old porcelain of the 'Compagnie
des Indes' must be considerable; there must be dining-room
canvases by Weenix and Hondecoeter, and perhaps some painted
rooms; but they should be searched more for old garden flowers,
it may be, than for old gardens. The pomologist might recover
many old kinds of pears and apples, including the mysterious,
pink-fleshed Dutch *poires d'amour*! But the old gardens, we fear,
are gone; and we can only turn to them in handcoloured prints
and drawings.*

* Further to the engraved views of Dutch gardens, already described,
we should mention *Het Zegepralende Kennemerlant* by Hendrik de Leth, 1730,
dealing with similar gardens in the district lying north of Haarlem. Simon
Schynvoet (1652–1727), an imposing figure in his periwig and with
aquiline features resembling those of his master William III, was the
architect who designed many of the gardens round The Hague, and along
the Rivers Vecht and Amstel. There is a book of engraved garden vases
by his hand, each in a background of high, clipped hedges. Jacques
Roman, another Dutch garden architect, worked at Het Loo; while Jan
van Call (*b*. The Hague, 1699) made the gardens at Klingendael.
Since this work was issued the country houses and gardens of the Vecht
have been the subject of a comprehensive study by Dr K. van Lutterveld,
under the title *De Buitenplaatsen aan de Vecht*, published by De Tijdsbroom,
Lochem.

9. Cornelis Troost and his times

To many persons enjoying the paintings in the Mauritshuis, a picture gallery of ideal size, neither too large, nor small, and containing an almost undue proportion of great masterpieces, one of the unexpected, unheralded delights will be the little corner room in which are hung the pastels or gouache drawings by Cornelis Troost. He has been called, without discrimination, the 'Dutch Watteau' or 'Dutch Hogarth', but he remains little studied and nearly, if not quite, unknown, nothing having been published with regard to him during that wide 'vulgarization' of knowledge between the two wars.* A few of his paintings are in the Rijksmuseum at Amsterdam, his native town, though their subjects, *An Anatomy Lesson, The Inspectors of the Collegium Medicum,* or *The Regents of the Aalmoezeniers-Weeshuis* (an orphanage), give but a small part of his talents. We may add that in England his paintings are confined to a single example in London, and to one or possibly two others in a private collection in Ireland. Troost is to be studied, therefore, at The Hague, with the proviso that he lived and died in Amsterdam.

His *forte* are his pastel paintings from Dutch comedies. These

* The exhibition of 'Cornelis Troost and His Times' held at the Boymans Museum, Rotterdam, in the summer of 1946, comprising thirty-four of his paintings and pastels and thirty-nine of his drawings from a wide variety of sources, together with the promise of a long deferred volume and catalogue *raisonné*, marked the beginnings of a wider fame. His individual and strongly marked drawings deserve attention, particularly in his interior scenes, in which he portrays figures and decorative details with a rapid handwriting and an observation all his own. Troost is one of the most individual of eighteenth-century draughtsmen.

are magical illusions or re-creations of life and manners during the early eighteenth century in Holland, the Confucian Age of Dutchmen when they were at the height of their material prosperity, or torpor, for it is not to be denied that they were exhausted from their heroic energies of the previous century and in the process of digesting or sleeping over their vast acquisitions in both Indies. But we will plunge, without more ado, into this magical peepshow of a forgotten world. In his gouache drawings, in which he is unique, we seem to catch, ever, in the distance, or not so far away, those sounds of laughter which are heard in the overture to 'Cosi Fan Tutte', but the comedy is not Italian, though, as we shall find, with Italian elements, and we will discover our way to it by looking, first, at the series of five drawings in the Mauritshuis in which Cornelis Troost is at his nearest to Hogarth and which, collectively, are given the name *Nelri,* a word coined from the first letters of the Latin inscriptions that accompany them. Like scenes from a play, they portray successive stages of conviviality in the house or club of Biberius, a name that sufficiently suggests the style of action. They are all of the same group of persons in the same interior, or in the same rooms, rather, for one of the scenes takes place in the dining-room that we see in the other drawings through the open door. The drama, therefore, is in the different attitudes of the figures and in the way the high-backed chairs are pushed back or moved around. The first scene, 'Nemo loquebatur' (the 'N' of *Nelri*), introduces us into just such an interior as we saw along the Keizersgracht or Heerengracht at Amsterdam, a room with pilasters and rich stucco ceiling, in which the party of Dutchmen are filling up or smoking at their long clay pipes, a scene by firelight and candlelight with a servant already uncorking bottles by a tall wine buffet in the corner. The next scene is wonderfully and minutely differenced, all the figures have moved their positions, and the wine is passing round. They are all a little drunken in the next drawing; a young man by the fireplace makes love to a pretty maidservant who holds a tray of glasses, and the rest of the company are arguing and disputing, and trying to locate from a map a place upon a globe; the double

22 *Middachte*

23   *Deventer*

doors into the room behind are now wide open, and we see the dining-room with a manservant laying the table, another room with stucco panels, a winecooler, and a glorious sideboard. Chairs are overturned, bottles thrown upon the floor, and the guests, in fact, are very drunk indeed. Lastly, we see them, maudlin, quarrelsome, half-asleep, standing up, reeling, in every stage of drunkenness, with the superscription, 'Ibant qui poterant, qui non potuere cadebant' ('Those, who could, went away, those who could not, fell down'). This set of drawings or gouache paintings do very nearly resemble the *Marriage à la Mode* of Hogarth; the lighter medium of gouache, is perhaps, more suited to the quick play of action, while the singular dexterity of Troost in handling the powdered chalk has enabled him to give a peculiar brilliance to such details as glasses and bottles, to shoes and waistcoats, to firelight and candlelight, and to the flickering play of figures within those tell-tale rooms.

This series of paintings of Dutch interiors, conceived and executed in a Hogarthian spirit, makes it an easy transference to the exterior life of Amsterdam, and here we may discover that the robuster Englishman, the Cockney painter who was born in Ship Court, Old Bailey, and who died in his house in Lincoln's Inn Fields, does not so well survive the journey down a few steps into the street, or the little, long, back garden. There is nothing of Watteau in Hogarth, and he is altogether lacking in the lighter graces. His streets and slums, his cockpits and election scenes, his *Beer Street,* and *Gin Lane,* are the expression of his satire and his sense of pity. We may suppose that, compared with London, Amsterdam was less crowded and less sordid. A painting by Cornelis Troost in the Teylers Museum, Haarlem, has for subject the street festival of the Three Kings, and shows the masquers with their Star of Bethlehem, a huge star-shaped lantern mounted upon a pole, singing outside a patrician house of Amsterdam. As compared with Hogarth, only a handful of persons is listening and watching in the deserted streets, but we would draw attention to a figure, shortly to become familiar, who stands apart, in 'peculiar' clothes and droll attitude, in the right hand corner. In

the Rijksmuseum there is a delightful little painting of a town
garden with a summer house or *gloriette* at the far end; the maid
in the foreground sits at her work, and at the back a gentleman on
a ladder cuts a bunch of grapes from a vine growing on the wall
and hands them to a little girl. In another painting, in a private
collection, a scene from a comedy, 'The Amorous Bregge', is being
played before a small audience in a summer garden. Wine and
fruit, and a great winecooler, are near by. The play is under the
full-leaved trees, close to a garden statue group of *The Rape of a
Sabine Woman*. We see the prompter with his book of words; the
audience sit on benches or smoke their long clay pipes sitting upon
the grass; and for immediate background there is a beautiful
pavilion fulfilling the place of painted architecture upon the
theatre scene. We would assign to this mood or group of paintings the beautiful picture that belonged to Mr Wyndham Clark.
It is of small size, in gouache, and represents a young married
couple visiting their parents in the country. An old inscription on
the back describes this as 'a capital picture of Dutch manners and
costume in the eighteenth century'. The country house is of typical
Dutch architecture. Both the façade and the gate piers are such
as we see in the villas along the Vecht, while the interior, we
might guess, would have cream and gilt doorways in the Rococo
manner, with grisaille paintings above, like those at the Huys Ten
Donck near Rotterdam.* In the Cornelis Troost picture – or
should we call it a drawing? – the coach-and-four has just driven
up to the front door, a coach drawn by four of the black Frisian
horses, probably from the isle of Ameland, the parents have come
out to greet them, and a servant leads away the horse on which
the husband has ridden all the way beside the carriage door. A
charming passage in this little picture is the pair of ladies embrac-
ing, in the centre foreground, in their yellow crinolines.

* Het Huis Ten Donck was begun by Otto Groeninx van Zoelen, Lord
of Ridderkerk, and Dijkgraaf of the polders of Oud and Nieuw Ryerwaard
in 1747, the year of the restoration of the House of Orange. It has beautiful
stucco work by an Italian, Pietro Castoldi, giving further proof that much
of the stucco in Dutch houses was by Italian craftsmen. An article on this
charming country house appeared in *Country Life* for 12th February 1938.

A daughter of the artist, Sarah Troost, who 'painted pastel portraits and made drawings from her father's pictures', married the collector and engraver, Ploos van Amstel, and it was he who published the large folio of engravings which included an illustration of a typical canal boat or *trekschuyt,* another perfect representation of Dutch manner and costume. The *trekschuyten* were the stage coaches of the Dutch canals, gloriously gilt and painted, fitted with every convenience including lavatories and smoking-rooms, and they must have formed one of the most pleasant and restful forms of locomotion there have ever been. But this painting may serve to remind us, too, of the Dutch pleasure parties on the water, when they floated along with wine and music under awnings made of lutestring.* A pair of engravings from the same huge folio are taken from paintings of revelry and merrymaking at an inn on the outskirts of Amsterdam, a place of popular resort upon summer evenings. The huge old inn, rather as in the *Nelri* series, is scenic backcloth for both paintings. It rises to its height with persons leaning out from every window. Below, the crowd of revellers is drinking and feasting in the spirit of a fair or *kermis,* but there are a pair of strangers at the feast, dressed alike, and at once we know them from their droll attitudes and 'peculiar' attire, exactly resembling that of the curious figure in the right-hand corner of that other painting. In that, their prototype stands with arms straight down in front of him, some distance away, as though shocked, yet fascinated, by the street festival of the Three Kings. But, in this pair of paintings, the two eccentrics have been drawn in and become the butt of all the revellers. They are sitting stiffly, side by side, upon a bench outside the inn door, refusing all alcoholic refreshment, or partaking of it in secret – who can tell? – but, certainly, in their black steeple hats, white collars and cuffs, and black, baggy breeches, they are sitting, not so much like a pair of skeletons as a couple of funeral mutes or undertakers at this allegro, and we use that word in its Miltonic import, of the burghers and shopkeepers of old Amsterdam. We shall meet

---

* Poetic licence, for, alas! it is a kind of silk material and not actual lutestring.

them, or their like, again; but, for the moment, let us keep the mystery.

It will bring us to his nine gouache paintings of Dutch comedies in the Mauritshuis, and to a few more in other collections out of the once existing, unknown total of such drawings. For they are, in fact, gouache drawings upon paper, and those now hanging in the Mauritshuis were bought at Amsterdam in 1829. Their subjects are scenes from old Dutch comedies, and in his theatrical paintings Cornelis Troost forms to himself, one of the most enchanting chapters of the whole eighteenth century. He is Dutch, entirely, yet with all the beauty of the Italian Comedy. His gouache is a lighter, quicker medium than the oil or canvas of de Wilde or Zoffany in their paintings of the London stage; it allows of the most brilliant finish to the details and incidentals, a fidelity of representation that is more appropriate and satisfying in coloured chalks than in oil, and that aids and perpetuates the stage illusion, to which end Troost, we shall notice, has a particular delight in white wall surfaces with the shadows of such objects as brooms or brushes or the pendulums of clocks in play upon them.* The double counterfeit of the object and its shadow had a fascination for him. But we observe that his comedies, and in this they differ in treatment from de Wilde or Zoffany, are not acted in the theatre. Troost chooses a situation and paints it in his own setting.

The Wedding of Kloris and Roosje, from a comedy by D. Buysero, shows the young couple dancing in the open air before a crowd of onlookers, and it is a scene of rustic merrymaking, not a stage picture. Only in the figures of Kloris and Roosje, who are obviously portraits, do we know that they are actors. We prefer, because it is entirely of the theatre, and of the Italian Comedy, at that, *The Deceived Lovers* from the farce, *Harlequin, Magician, and Barber* by W. van der Hoeven, introducing Belloardo, 'a half-mad physician', and Capitano, a 'bragging military man',

---

* A painting with curious analogy to Cornelis Troost in manner and technique is that by Giovanni da San Giovanni (1590–1636), the Florentine mannerist, of a scene outside an inn, in the Palazzo Pitti.

rivals of his master for the fair Sophia, the old set characters of the *Commedia dell' Arte,* and, in fact, Harlequin is shaving one of his victims in the street outside a barber's shop, and throwing powder in his eyes, but the houses are Dutch, there is one of the tree-lined canals of Amsterdam for background, and in the chequers of Harlequin the broad humour of the Dutch *kermesse* mingles with the light and shade of Bergamo. *The Old Husband Driven out of Doors,* from the farce, *Hopman Ulrich,* depicts an incident which may not have been particularly funny in itself, but Troost has made it the occasion for a sparkling rendering of detail in a firelit interior with candles burning on the table and the chimneypiece, a brush standing in the fireplace, a pair of tongs lying on the floor, a bottle and glasses, the flowered dressing gown of the old husband, and, above all, the array of blue and white Delft vases on a tall cupboard, and the walls of embossed and painted leather which have a pattern like the floreated back, many times repeated, of a 'Chippendale' chair. *The Quarrel of the Astronomers,* from another old farce, takes place in an inn at Loenen, among the villas of the river Vecht, and portrays the two learned doctors disputing the solar systems of Ptolemy and Copernicus and illustrating their argument with the help of the dishes and bottles of their dinner table.

But it is in the scenes taken from burgher or peasant comedies that Cornelis Troost excels himself, in the vaudevilles, that is to say, of Thomas Asselyn and Abraham Alewijn. In the 1946 exhibition of 'Cornelis Troost and His Times', at Rotterdam, there was a splendid gouache drawing, from a private collection, of the courtroom scene from *t'Beslikte Zwaentje,* by the latter playwright, a plain whitewashed room with raftered ceiling, the white wall playing the part of screen or transparency, for it silhouettes the action. Upon that wall, for our delight in textures, Troost has painted in gouache several pictures hanging over the door, a shelf of blue and white Delft below that, an antlered deer's head, and in the alcove one of the Frisian cuckoo clocks from Loure with the cords of the pendulum and their lines of shadow. The bewigg'd lawyer, with his hat on, is as sinister as the lawyers of Daumier or

Forain, the magistrate is another giant of a man, while the culprits and their accusers, and the public in court, are all closely observed and could mostly, or all, be the likenesses of well-known actors.

Jan Claesz, or the Disguised Servant, an old comedy by Thomas Asselyn, 1680, seems to have been a favourite subject with Cornelis Troost. There are three scenes from *Jan Claesz* in the Mauritshuis, and a couple more on exhibition in the picture gallery at Utrecht. It is in these that we meet again with the drolls or 'peculiar persons', and the plot of the play reveals their identity and tells us who they are. In the first painting of the series in the Mauritshuis, Saartje Jans, who is secretly engaged to Jan Claesz, is visited in her father's house by two men in black who sit awkwardly, side by side, in their tall steeple hats, their hands upon their knees, and who have come to ask her father to grant her hand in marriage to their friend, Reinier Adriaensz. They are a pair of Quakers. In the next painting Reinier confesses his love to Saartje Jans, and is mocked by her. There follows her stratagem to introduce her lover Jan Claesz, disguised as a servant girl, into her father's house where he enjoins 'her' to take good care of Saartje and sleep in her room in order to protect her from Jan Claesz. We will follow the plot no further, but return to the first of the paintings and to the 'peculiar persons' sitting side by side, for this is the most successful of the theatrical paintings by Cornelis Troost, and while entirely of the theatre it gives us a picture of the incomparable richness and diversity of life in eighteenth-century Holland, of what we would call 'Confucian' Holland, Dutch conservatism which kept the forms of earlier centuries almost into modern times. The light of the canals is reflected on those whitewashed walls as background for the pair of drolls or zanies, who in this setting become like an addition of new characters to the *Commedia dell' Arte.* This is a little masterpiece of painting, and there is a physical delight to be had in its inconceivable neatness of rendering.

Our remarks on Cornelis Troost and his times, a neglected period in Dutch art history, are not complete without mention of the pastels of Liotard, a Genevan, who is famed principally for his portraits in Oriental costume drawn in Turkey and in Moldavia, but who worked in The Hague, Delft, and Amsterdam in 1755–7, and again at The Hague in 1771–2, and left descendants who lived in Holland. His masterpiece, the portrait of Mary Gunning, Countess of Coventry, seated in a Turkish dress upon a divan, hangs in the Rijksmuseum, the legacy of a Mademoiselle Liotard in 1873, and much like a Degas in drawing and technique, while a number of his pastel portraits are still in private hands in Holland. The French pastellist, J. B. Perronneau, worked, and is said to have died, in Amsterdam in 1783, and there are portraits by him, too, in Dutch collections. There are good portraits, in oil, also, by J. F. A. Tischbein, a German painter, though born at Maastricht, who worked at The Hague in 1786, and later.

Here may be mentioned what could be described as a minor work of art of the first order, and a document relevant to the Dutch influence abroad. It is one of the 60 odd paintings in the Rijksmuseum by J. B. Vanmour (1671–1737), a native of Valenciennes who settled in Constantinople in 1699, spent his life in the Levant, and became the foremost of the painters of the Bosphorus. This collection was formed by the Dutch Ambassador Cornelis Calkoen, and for the most part they are small paintings of Turkish types and costumes, but there is, also, a portrait of the Ambassador, and there are three large paintings of the reception of the Dutch Embassy by Achmet III. It was under this Sultan that Turkish extravagance in costume was carried to its furthest lengths, and his reign has been called 'The Tulip Reign' because of the tulip festivals held by the Sultan and his ministers, the flower having a particular attraction for the Turks, owing to its resemblance to their turbans. The paintings represent the Ambassador Cornelis Calkoen crossing the second court of the Old Seraglio at the moment when the Janissaries rushed for their dinners, which were laid out from them under the plane trees upon their kettle-drums, a ceremony intended to impress foreigners with their fierceness; the banquet given by the Grand Vizir in the Hall of the

Divan; and the reception of the Ambassador by the Sultan. It is the second of these paintings that we describe. The Dutch Ambassador and his suite, wearing their robes of honour, are seated on low benches along the walls. Above, behind a grille or latticed window, unseen, the Sultan is watching them. It is a charming pavilion in Turkish Rococo, built in 'The Tulip Reign', the prettiest interior of that grim old palace. Nowhere else in the world is there to be found such a representation of the fantastic pantomime costumes of the Old Seraglio. The servitors, in their long robes, wear high conical hats of different forms which we might consider to have come down in unbroken descent from the priests of Isis and Osiris. We see the Dutchmen in their large periwigs, perhaps a little old fashioned in their time, but the representatives of the greatest nation of merchants and traders of their day, and it is a fascination to think of them in so close a proximity to the Kislar or Capou Aghassi, Chiefs of the Black or White Eunuchs, to the *peyks* with their bows and arrows and headdresses of ostrich plumes, to the porters or *bostandjis,* to the gardeners with their tall mitres, half an ell in height, to the tressed halberdiers, and to the hidden beauties of the third court or harem.

We would speak, now, for the moment is propitious, of Rombout Verhulst (1624-98), the greatest of the Dutch sculptors. He studied in Italy, but lived chiefly at The Hague, and is known primarily for his monuments to Dutch admirals, to van Tromp in the Oudekerk at Delft, and to de Ruyter in the Nieuwekerk at Amsterdam. These are of a pattern, and the best part of them is the relief of a naval battle on a marble panel below the effigy. More tombs of admirals, by Verhulst, are, no no, *were* in the Grootekerk at Rotterdam; and they become monotonous. But Rombout Verhulst was capable of better things; his tomb, for instance, at Stavenisse on the far point of Tholen, in Zeeland, to Hieronymus van Tuyll van Serooskerken; or at Midwolde on the border of Groningen, in the far north of The Netherlands, an enormous funerary sculpture to a nobleman and his wife, with a background of heraldic shields in dozens, no less, the personages being Karel Hieronymus, Baron van Innhausen and Kniphausen, and his wife

Anna van Ewsum,* who, later, married her brother-in-law, whose statue in armour is at the foot of the monument. Henri Havard, a Frenchman to the core, is reminded, by the statue of her first husband, of 'that magnificent bust, by Rotrou, we all so admired in the lounge of the Comédie Française'. This is, probably, the most imposing and beautiful of Dutch monuments, showing much the same Italian influence that is to be noted in the English sculptor, Nicholas Stone, the accent of Bernini in a heavier, Northern tongue. Another monument, that to the Admiral Jonan van Brakell in the Grootekerk once at Rotterdam, speaks the same language though it is by a different sculptor, J. Bloemendael, and is even more Baroque in treatment. The eighteenth century in Holland, we would say in conclusion, is singularly lacking in funerary monuments.

In the space at our disposal, it is impossible to follow, as we would have liked, the development of Dutch furniture and interior decoration, and we can only point to the splendid room in 'Adam' style in the Rijksmuseum, that came from a house at Haarlem. We may note that the carpet, apparently a fine Savonnerie, is as likely to have been woven in the Chenille factory in Belgium. Nothing can be said of Delft pottery and tiles, even of such technical masterpieces as the blue and white violin in the Rijksmuseum,

---

* In the *Almanach de Gotha*, it is indicated that the ancient family of van Innhausen-en-Kniphausen, 'Maison des chefs de tribus de la Frise', or, in fact, of ancient Frisian origin, often bear the Christian name of 'Dodo', and not only 'Dodo', but 'Tido' too. The late prince (*b.* 1876) was Dodo-Charles-Tido-Albert-Edzard. The family estates, are, or were, on the borders of Oldenburg and Hanover; but, also, they were possessed of *biens allodiaux* on the Isle of Rügen where they were neighbours to the Princes (Fürst und Herren) of Putbus, an ancient family, now extinct in the male line, who are lineal descendants of the ancient kings of Rügen, and proprietors of this Baltic island with its high chalk cliffs. 'Buried in the recesses of a mysterious grove lies the Hertha-See, called the Black Lake from the dark shadows of the beechwoods. Tactius (*Germ.* c. 40) describes an untrodden wood (*castum nemus*) in which the car of the goddess Hertha was kept, drawn by cows, and washed in a secret lake.' From this remote island was Rome overthrown after an existence of twelve centuries. Odoacer, who finally captured the Roman capital, was King of Rügen, and ancestor of the Prince of Putbus.

painted with scenes of music in an interior. But we must spare a line or two for the incomparable Dutch silver. There were, as we have seen, great silversmiths at Leeuwarden in Friesland, with a particular or provincial manner of their own. Yet more individual were the van Vianen family, silversmiths of Utrecht, with their strange repertory of sea monsters and marine forms. Paulus van Vianen was the earliest of the family, dying before 1620, while his brother Adam was not less celebrated. The forte of the two brothers was mythological scenes in repoussé or deep relief. Christiaan, the son of Adam van Vianen, something of a Jacques Callot or a della Bella in the white metal, was called to England by Charles I, where he made silver vessels for St George's Chapel, Windsor, which were melted down in the Commonwealth. Another silversmith working in the same manner, Jan Lutma, was the friend of Rembrandt. These works in silver, in an ultra-Baroque style, are something unique to Holland and to them there is no parallel in other lands.

And we would end with the Dutch drinking glasses engraved with the diamond point, a gossamer sub-art of fragile nature, of which the masters were Frans Greenwood and D. Wolff. As an art it appears to have been largely in the hands of amateurs, sometimes of the female sex, as in the case of the *roemers* of green glass engraved by Anna Roemer Visscher and the glasses of Anna Maria van Schuurman, a lady whom we have met in the course of this work in other spheres. Frans Greenwood (1680-1761), perhaps of English parentage, made use of figures from the Italian Comedy by Jacques Callot and of Dutch genre subjects by Ostade or Teniers; while David Wolff, a little later in date (1732-98), worked in stipple engraving and drew portraits and figures of cupids or *amorini*. The long flute glasses are among the most beautiful Dutch examples of this art; but, to speak in general terms, there are beautiful specimens of the calligraphic style, bold interlacing flourishes and initials; there are wreaths or borders of flowers, roses, lilies, and fritillaries; the glasses by famous masters which may combine the line and stipple techniques; while a special word must be reserved for the rendering of coats-of-arms and heraldry, and for the exquisite diamond point engravings of ships in full sail. These latter are, perhaps, the most lovely of all Dutch glasses, and as it should be, are at their most beautiful when filled with wine.

10. Zeeland

The islands of Schouwen and Tholen, Noord and Suid Beveland, Walcheren; Zeeuwsch – Vlaandaren, Over Flakkee and Voorne.

It will not be lost upon the discerning reader that the author of this book had a particular affection and interest for Friesland and for the little dead towns on the far side of the Zuyder Zee, and that this was not so much renewed as born again after seeing them once more in April of 1973. But the other magnet that drew him again to Holland was the possibility of visiting Zeeland. In 1947 towns like Middelburg had been so badly damaged in the Second World War, and were even so difficult of access that a proposed visit to them was called off. So the final chapter of the book was concocted from what I could discover about the islands, without going to them, supplemented by Harry Batsford who did get there and supplied voluminous notes. Now, therefore, this last chapter is remodelled from personal experience still fresh in my mind, while retaining anything pertinent and of interest from what was there before.

We set forth from The Hague with a car and driver kindly supplied by the Netherlands Ministry of Foreign Affairs at about ten o'clock in the morning, and soon were passing the impressive and immense docks of Rotterdam which indeed are on a scale only comparable to the London docks. Having been there on the previous day, which was a Sunday, in order to see the Boymans Museum, it was difficult to credit that this was once a town of fine old houses second only to those of Amsterdam and The Hague. But in fact on this occasion we only skirted the town and were passing docks and derricks for more than a half hour on end.

At last and somewhere in the direction of Dordrecht, we were free of them and starting upon the extraordinary series of bridges and embankments that have transformed the approach to these islands in the last few years. Till this happened, and it came only gradually, it was a journey by steamer and ferry that took many hours; and of course if you wanted to visit the individual islands, Schouwen and Tholen, and North and South Beveland, separately and for their own sakes, it would be a matter of allowing for several days. Now, along bridge and causeway, one can get from The Hague to Flushing at the far side of Walcheren in under four hours.

The first island reached, and still not part of Zeeland, is Over Flakkee of which there is little to remember, and here the monotony grows rather more than remarkable. How is it possible that these endless flat meadows can ever have been interesting? But we cross into Schouwen and are on the fringe of yet another Arcadia of the rich peasant farmers and local patrician families; Zeeland being a world of its own, enclosed and interlaced with waters, extending to some 40 miles in length and breadth, but containing within that area as many as five or six distinct cultures or independent existencies, each divided again into the two separate worlds of Protestant or Catholic. The province consists of five islands, Walcheren, right out in the North Sea, Noord and Suid Beveland like causeways leading to it, and above them Schouwen and Tholen. Like far off Friesland, these isles were paradises of the farmers and rich peasants until the turn of the century. We would see it, not now, nor in the Middle Ages, but at some time not long ago when it was quite unspoilt, when the persons you met had passed their whole lives in one island, crossing, at most by painted sleigh from Schouwen, it might be, into Tholen, which was another world as far to them as Italy or Spain, or, for the rest, driving to market or to the *Kermesse* in their painted wagons, walking to church on Sundays, and on Sunday afternoons shooting with longbows at the target on the village green. Let it be said that those persons who love old, lost worlds and low horizons with no mountains, must rejoice in Zeeland.

Schouwen was rich in madder and in soda. This was its wealth. And we would choose to have seen it on a winter day when the rich farmers crossed from Schouwen into Duiveland in their sleighs. This was the paradise noted down and seen by Maaskamp in 1798, who says of the costumes that 'they were a pleasure and a curiosity to behold'. The sleigh would be painted light blue and white, with red runners. The farmer who pushes it across the snow has a black felt hat, black corduroy breeches, many silver buttons, and a jacket – waistcoat of glazed damask with a Persian design of yellow, dark green and crimson, and black flowers upon grass-green. And the lady of the sleigh? She wears a scallop hat of straw, probably from Luton, lined with red, gold corkscrews in her hair, and two pairs of ribbon streamers *à la* Bird of Paradise (more than one species of Bird of Paradise indulges itself in this fantasy of head or tail streamers!). She has a shoulder cape of flowered mauve cotton, and a camlet skirt of blue. We read that the camlet skirts of Schouwen and Duiveland were finer in colour and texture than those worn in the other islands. And they are gone, in the very moment, in that pale blue sleigh over the endless snow.

For the present there is positively nothing more to see. No wonder though that the local inhabitants were at pains to make their own lives interesting. This island of Schouwen had its primitive painter Marinus van Romerswaele, the Marinus de Zeeuw of the old writers, the Dutch for sailor or sea-lander being *de Zeeuw*, while Marinus is no more than the Latinized form of sea-lander or sailor, but this amphibian-sounding painter seems to have been a pupil of Quentin Matsys. His creepily realistic paintings of St Jerome in contemplation have a curious individuality of their own; Philip II collected his pictures, as he did those of Hieronymus Bosch, and they are to be seen at the Escorial, a world apart from his birthplace, Zierickzee.

And now the incredible is happening. After some two hours or more we are arriving somewhere. And where else would it be but this very Zierickzee that I had so much longed to see! And indeed it is one of the prettiest places imaginable. We turn a corner and are outside the ancient gate tower of the town where lives the burgomaster, and are at the head of a wide canal flanked by lovely old houses on both its banks. It is true there is only one Venice, but there are other lovely water towns as well, if hardly another in which every house is beautiful as at Zierickzee. They are of all periods, from early medieval up to early nineteenth century, a lot of the later ones having the elaborate and imaginative fanlights or overdoors that are such a feature of eighteenth-century Holland.

After luncheon in the hotel, which is in one of such houses, and a paragon of cleanliness even for its own homeland, we were shown by the burgomaster over the tower which is his residence; and were then taken by him to the Stadhuis or town hall where we saw the marriage-room with delightful grisaille paintings by M. Jos. Geeraerts (1707-91), a painter from Antwerp, who must have passed a pleasant life wandering among these islands for he worked too in the Oost-Indische Companie house at Middelburg. On the top floor of the Stadhuis is a room with showcases in which are displayed the beautiful local costumes, only just installed, being probably the only and last specimens to be found. And, as well, one of the beautiful and imaginative sledges of Zeeland. There are also, if I am not mistaken, specimens of the local clocks to compare with those of Friesland. And after a final tour of the town, with old houses innumerable, an Arcadian outdoor or summer fish market, and a last look at the canal of Zierickzee, bucolic equal and counterpart to the more celebrated Rapenburg of Leyden, we left for Veere.

Characteristically, though, as it seemed to me, we were starting backwards, going in the opposite direction to that I had imagined. But this was a question of crossing from Schouwen to Noord Beveland, so let us be thinking of Noord and Suid Beveland which we are traversing on our way to Walcheren where

Veere is situate. And as there is nothing to see, meanwhile, let us listen to what the Frenchman Henri Havard in 1878 has to say of these islands! He was particularly delighted with Werneldingen a small village of Zuid Beveland which he describes as 'resembling a big box of Nuremberg toys just unpacked; a double row of dwellings, all painted in vivid colour, all built in exactly the same way, with straw-coloured woodwork, planted with two rows of little old trees, all clipped, shaped, and pointed, forming a kind of screen, no thicker or higher at one end than the other, nor in the middle than at the two ends. The young women of Werneldingen might easily be taken for large dolls, perfectly new, quite uninjured, just taken out of boxes in which they have been packed so carefully that their complexions are not injured, nor their dresses crushed'. Upon the morning Havard saw them, the young girls wore 'all white and pink, all dressed exactly alike, and each with a flower in her mouth'.

Havard was enchanted with their costume, and this we supplement with a mention of their immense lace caps, their fichus of flowered silk, gold head-bands, and black damask skirts. But, more than all else, it is their coral necklaces. The Protestant women of the island wear necklaces of five rows of coral beads; while the Catholic have lace caps like those worn by the nuns of Bruges and 'chokers' of six rows of corals. Not so long before this the costumes were more glorious still, for it is of Zuid Beveland that Maaskamp remarks, writing in 1798: 'Crossing over from the islands Walcheren and Schouwen to that of Zuid Beveland, we meet here with peasants and countrywomen, of whom it may properly be said: "These people are entirely of gold and silver".' One of the plates in *The National Costumes of Holland* gives us the glitter of their amazing dresses. A young bourgeois woman is in a *schulphold* or 'scallop' hat of straw with an enchanting flowered chintz to line it, red ribbons to tie it under her chin, and four flowered ribbons hanging from the brim, two to either side of her face. Her *beuk,* or chest-covering, is of blue flowered chintz; her bodice of shiny damask with a Persian pineapple in black upon it; she has ribbons crisscrossing her waist of brocaded silk in gold, red, and silver upon blue. She has a brown damask skirt with white flowers all over it, and a linen apron, striped black, scarlet, purple, yellow, white, and green. Her elbowed sleeves are of flowered brocade, light yellow edged with pale blue and white braid, and she has mittens to her elbows of knitted white and yellow silk; or in winter they are of chamois leather embroidered in white silk; she has a bag and a châtelaine on silver chains. The man wears a black silk beaver hat, with black ribbons, black corduroy breeches, and knots of coloured ribbons at his knees. His glory in his waistcoat-jacket of green glazed damask, flowered with two shades of yellow, two shades of red, blue and white.

And in no more time than it takes to read these paragraphs we arrive at Veere which lies on the narrow inlet of sea between Noord Beveland and Walcheren. Veere is older of aspect than Zierickzee and has more medieval houses. It is also a much smaller town. How curious to think that like Amalfi, like Salerno, it had a distinct maritime history and by *esprit de contradiction,* not, as one might think with England which lies opposite to Veere, but with Scotland. Hence, the pair of Scottish houses, Het Lammerje (1539) and de Struys (1561) which were once ware-houses and offices of the Scots wool merchants then active in Veere. And trading with where? With the little port of Culross upon the Firth of Forth maybe, except that it was a Hansa trading post; but in any case with ports of about its own size with perhaps not more than 2,000 or 3,000 inhabitants at its heyday. The connection of Veere with Scotland continued over perhaps two centuries or more; it being stated that as late as 1805 Scotland sent an ambassador, or, at the least, an emissary of some degree to Veere, but by that time its prosperity was on the decline. At its zenith, Wolfaert van Borselen, a local nobleman, married Mary, daughter of James VI (1566–1625) of Scotland. It is curious for an Englishman to think of the Scots, who if not hereditary enemies were certainly not friends, established in this little for-gotten town. One can even think to hear their distinctive accent on the cobbled streets. There is not much else in Veere but the Stadhuis in elaborate late Flemish guise; more that than Dutch I

thought. It dates from 1474, the work of the same architect who
designed the Middelburg town hall, and has a slim and graceful tower, surmounted by a many-staged carillon-loud, bulbous
steeple. And after friendly converse with the burgomaster of Veere,
who dined with us that same night at Goes, we were on our way to
Middelburg in the centre of Walcheren, no more than a few
minutes' drive away.

At Middelburg, again, the quantity of fine old houses is an
astonishment. They are mainly of the seventeenth and eighteenth
centuries which was the time of prosperity, as one may judge
from walking along the Londense Kaai, the Bier Kaai, the
Rouaanse or the Rotterdamse Kaai, names that are their own
explanation.* The elaborate water 'lay-out' of Middelburg, as
complicated if regular of outline as a starfish, has survived but the
huge old Premonstratensian Abbey has suffered badly. Perhaps
this was never very beautiful, but the Kloveniersdolen, club of the
musketeers, the St Joris Doelen, club of the crossbowmen, both of
the late sixteenth century, are gone. We think, also, of the Oost-
Indische Huis and warehouses of the Companie te Middelburg,
both of the next century – for Zeeland had its own East India
Company – tall red brick buildings, both with pediments, the
latter boasting the figure of a plumed 'Indian' in copper, upon
the cornice, turning in the trade wind on an armillary sphere.
There were lovely houses, too, in Middelburg of the eighteenth
century – the Provincial Library, once a patrician house, and the
work almost certainly of Daniel Marot; of this the stones have been
carefully preserved and it is rebuilding, we were informed; other
houses in pleasant simple Rococo, it is said by an architect from
Antwerp, also survive, fronting the canal with its factories and
incongruous row of booth-shops. The beauty of Middelburg, we
reiterate, was its streets of old houses and its costumed peasants
during the Kermesse, or upon market days. Indeed, a number of
old houses of the three Renaissance centuries have come through

* A beautiful three-floor, nine-windowed house with balconied overdoors typical of the local Middelberg style is at Gortekaar 30. It now
contains an excellent restaurant.

the ordeal, and curiously enough they accord well with the tide of new buildings all around them. The houses on the great market square have been largely reconstructed, but bridal couples till only a few years ago were still taken to the photographers in a delightful little eighteenth-century chariot with polished wooden panels, and there is a fine hearse with black Baroque carving.

There is, or was, in Middelburg, an equivalent to the Frisian Museum at Leeuwarden, named, simply enough, the Zeeuwsch Genootschap der Wetenschappen, and containing rooms decorated in the old Zeeland style.* It is upon these interiors from old houses and their figures that we have to base our observations on the dress of Walcheren, aided by the never-failing *National Costumes of Holland* – before we leave Middelburg for the Arcadian countryside around it, we would remind ourselves that Walcheren for all its remoteness was in communication with the greater world outside it. It could be said, indeed, that Europe was divided into East and West from Walcheren, for it was at the castle of Oost-Sonbourg, in September 1556, that the Emperor Charles v separated the Habsburg dominions, abdicating Spain, the Low Countries, Naples, and the Indies (Mexico and Peru), to his son Philip ii, while his own brother Ferdinand, King of the Romans, inherited the Imperial purple and became Holy Roman Emperor. It was the greatest division of power for over 1,000 years, since Valens and Valentinian divided the Roman Empire into East and West. Charles v, a few months later, sailed from Flushing to die in his lonely cloister at Yuste, in Estremadura. We must remember, also, the close contact between Middelburg and France as shown in the wine steeple set up for the 'white wines of France and the red wines of Gascony'. The *Wijnheeren* or wine merchants were the richest of the guilds of Middelburg, and the quay of Rouen (Rouaansohe Kaai) is still existing. The French merchants lived at Arnemuiden, another little old decaying sea-port, where their

* The entire collection of Zeeland costumes from the Zeeuws Museum is now in the restored Abbey of Middelburg, properly arranged and ready for inspection.

ships put in; and there, also, were the 'nation of Brittany', or Breton merchants from St Malo. There was trade, as well, from England, Scotland, with the councillors and traders of the 'nation of Lucca', that 'of the coast of Biscay and province of Guipuzcoa', 'of the nation of the sea-coast of Spain', the 'nation of Venetia', the 'Portuguese nation', and the 'nation of Andalusia'. But the internal prosperity of Walcheren, which till the religious wars was rivalling that of Bruges, as distinct from the wealth brought into it by ships, consisted in its fisheries, its cornlands, and in its flocks and herds, as could be seen from the paintings of oxen adorned with garlands in the Gothic meat market under one side of the Town Hall.

The modern port of Flushing, on the other side of Walcheren, much damaged in the War, had an eighteenth-century Stadhuis, once a 'patrician' house, 'Anno 1730' writ large upon it, more suited to Syracuse or Trapani than Flushing with its pair of female busts placed as though looking out through the attic windows, its coat-of-arms in the pediment, and its roof line crowded with statues of Neptune in his sea-chariot flanked with a pair of goddesses to either side. We may like or dislike this building according to taste, but it is more interesting to recall that Constantin Guys, the draughtsman of the Second Empire in so many of its aspects, was born at Flushing in 1813 during the wars of Napoleon, his father being Chief Commissioner of the French Navy. A tall, typical fretted steeple, the St Jacobstoren, and a street of old houses have been spared, ranging above a sea-wall of Vauban-like falsifications; and beyond, the dunes loom dark, and in the dusk almost cliff-like, north-westward to West Kapelle, Walcheren's farthest point.

But away to the milk-pails and the tilted carts! The little town of Arnemuiden, aforementioned, is one of the places in Walcheren, or indeed in all Holland, that has preserved something of its ancient costume, the particular feature of the Zeeland women's costumes being the *beuk* or square chest-covering, and the different forms of cap. Every village has its own form of cap and it is this, rather than the peaked cap of Volendam, that is really typical of Dutch costume. With it is worn most elaborate jewellery, comprising the *krullen* or gold corkscrews, ending in bangles, that hang above the eyes. It is a dress associated with blue milk-pails, and with the covered wagons of Zeeland, still gaily painted, if not as brightly, or as many in number, as before. Many are, or were, its variations. The question of where the women tied their aprons, higher or lower upon their waist; and there were villages such as West-kapelle whose inhabitants never intermarried with other villages, and who were said to be of Scandinavian descent. Another form of dress worn by the farmers' wives, and in which they drove to market in their painted wagons, was remarkable for its coal-scuttle straw bonnets, adaptations of those worn by the women of Antwerp or other Flemish towns in the '30s and '40s of last century; but with what invention! For the straw hats which were brimless and worn with white cambric undercaps, had broad blue throat-ribbons or *keslinten* hanging down from them, down to the waist, of blue broché satins, or even of white broché worked with coloured flowers. These ribbons had gold clips to fasten them; but from the back of the straw hat there fluttered another pair of ribbons, only for ornament, and of violet, blue, or orange silk. With this they wore the *krullen* or golden corkscrews on their temples; and across their foreheads the golden *naald* pointing to the right if married, and if unmarried pointing the other way. Black aprons, striped skirts, three petticoats on week-days, and seven upon Sundays; and in winter the *Labadisten* (*vide ante* p. 123) or wool-mittens.

But the most charming of the Walcheren dresses figured in the *National Costumes of Holland,* is still more curious in origin. The ladies of the old noble families of this island, living in their country houses, followed – at a distance – the Paris fashions, and the farmers and peasants imitated them, but yet more behind. Now during the last years of the eighteenth century, the French under the influence of Jean-Jacques Rousseau and in the shadow of the coming Revolution, were inspired by their own peasant fashions. So it came about that the country families of Walcheren must have appeared in these artful simplicities of fashion; and then, some years later, they were imitated and improved upon by their own tenants, just in the years when that Arcadia flowed with milk and honey, and they were able to afford the most expensive materials and any quantity of gold jewellery. The young women's dress, thus inspired, is of utmost fascination, and just such as we would imagine for an Arcadian isle.

The one of them depicted wears a lace cap, of the sort of lace called *potten Kant,* with a design of lilies in vases, or, sometimes, birds, and a silver *naald* pointing downwards in the centre of her forehead to denote she is neither married, nor even engaged. This maiden, thus sealed and delivered, has a shallow straw hat of delicious curve with a small flat brim, lined with a flowered chintz, and tied with black ribbons underneath her chin. These are the straw-hats which, we have said before, are among the most poetical inventions of the peasant mind. And it has two streamers of brocaded ribbon hanging from it, green, bright pink, purple, and red with an indented or waved edge. She wears a neckerchief or fichu of checked linen in two shades of red, and a bodice of blue flowered chintz with a pattern of formal carnations or pinks upon it. Her short skirt is of pinkish purple and black damask with an Oriental pattern, and she wears a striped taffeta apron that, as our authority points out, is entirely Louis XVI in feeling. It has long, thin muslin panels. That is how it looks, patterned with flowers, and between them, long, thin, flowered strips in several colours, green, and yellow, and bright red. Her skirt and apron stand out boldly, for she has padded hips; she has a brocade bag fastened to her waist upon a silver chain; and we can only say of this milkmaid or shepherdess, with her shallow straw hat lined with chintz, her coloured streamers and her striped apron, that her dress has the beauty of a country poem, but a poem written by a voluptuary who has known the town.

Her partner, and we must describe him quickly, is dressed in black, and is a delayed version of the bucks and dandies of St James's Street. Black, curled hair (for like many of the Zeelanders he shows the signs of Spanish blood), a silk beaver hat with narrow brim, curled up behind and down in front. A ribbon of black flowered petersham round his 'barrel' hat, and gold earrings. A short black coat and kneebreeches; knots of coloured ribbons at his knees, and a damask waistcoat woven of four threads. It is of yellow and green flowers upon a scarlet ground; but, in general, this top-hatted paragon with his petersham band and shining earrings would wear green damask for the *Kermis,* blue for his wedding day, and scarlet and yellow upon Sundays, for feast days, or if a prince or princess of the House of Orange was visiting Walcheren.

Departing eastward from that isle and looking backwards – as who would not, for such figures are no longer of the world we live in? – we are in Zuid Beveland, of which the capital is the little town of Goes, a name that is pronounced rustically and endearingly, like that of the parent of the golden egg, or, more exactly, like the Scots version of 'house' and that will recall to us, if nothing else, the painter Hugo van der Goes, born according to one account at Ghent, but, in the words of another, 'Hughe van der Ghoest in Zeeland was so called because he lived long in that country'. His masterpiece is the magnificent triptych in the Uffizi Gallery at Florence,* completed about 1475 and painted to the order of Portinari, agent of the Medici in Bruges. The picture seems to have gone direct from Bruges to Florence. About 1475, or a little later, Goes joined his own brother as a lay brother in a cloister near Brussels, but continued to paint and receive important visitors. In 1480, or thereabouts, he went to Louvain to value the estate of the painter Dieric Bouts, and then to Cologne on which journey he was seized by madness or religious melancholia and died, still insane, the following year. His association with Goes seems, indeed, a little tenuous. Whatever the facts, no one who has seen it will ever forget this painting, with its elongated

* Another triptych by Hugo van der Goes, of the Madonna and child with S. S. Catherine and Barbara, is – or was! – in the church of the Gesú at Polizzi la Generosa in Sicily, inland from Cefalú. But is it by van der Goes? I have never seen it illustrated; and in any case is the painting still *in situ?* It is said to have been in freight on a vessel which was wrecked on the coast some miles away.

northern figures at the back and the marvellous jug of irises in the foreground.

Goes, where we were to spend the night, is a pleasant little market town, with a vast open square of peaceful, even somnolent aspect, though the heaps of all kinds of household goods piled against the walls of the great fast-closed church the day before showed that it can be lively enough on market day. We had in fact taken much trouble and gone there deliberately for the Tuesday night in order to see the market next morning. Over and over again one reads that 'the rustic inhabitants of the neighbourhood in their national costume are to be seen on market day', or words to that effect. But alas! the only trace of the costume left are the *krullen* or golden corkscrews worn on the women's temples, and soon those will be gone too. The great four-aisled church of St Mary Magdalene is outstanding for the graceful design of the almost curvilinear tracery of its immense windows. At the back it composes strikingly with the Stadhuis, where a late brick tower has been incorporated, not incongruously into a Louis xv façade. The organ in the church has painted shutters, and above them, a canopied and curtained proscenium with figures of angel musicians in the manner of the peepshows at the *Kermis*! And nearby in the square a shapely Rococo stone façade houses the Korenbeurs Hotel which is exceptional for its comfort and good food. It occupies what must have been the finest house in Goes, and Napoleon and the Empress Marie Louise stayed here for some time in 1811 when she was *enceinte* with l'Aiglon, the King of Rome. Impossible not to think of his strange and tragic destiny when woken by the carillon in the early morning!

Next day the market stalls were erecting with much hammering and talking; but not a sign of the costumes. Yet the *National Costumes of Holland,* only as late as 1932 reports that the folk of Goes set the fashions for the whole of Zeeland; in the little town is seen the wide 'butterfly-wing' lace caps, but on the way to Middelburg, a matter of half a dozen miles, no more, is found a small close-fitting type, worn on the back of the head, with a little overcap of blue. Roundabout Goes two small rectangular gilt plates project from the *oorijzer*, or gold or silver headdress, rather in the fashion of motor-mirrors. Often from the inverted cork-screw *oorijzer* hang dangling filigree ornaments, frequently triangular, and filigree-headed pins fasten the hair inside. The five-row necklace of coral beads is universal, with a large gilt metal clasp in front. These were once obtainable in the jewellers' shops but in 1973 there was not a sign of them. The whole of that living past in the present time is gone, what with the Second World War, television, and the internal combusion engine. And we left Goes a little sadly for the other extremity of Holland where we were to reach Leeuwarden, capital of Friesland, and alternate Arcadia of the Hollanders, by nightfall.

But Harry Batsford, my companion on the previous journey in 1947, penetrated farther into Zeeland, in fact to Zeeusch-Vlanderen, that narrow strip of sand on the south bank of the Scheldt, 40 miles in length, nowhere more than 10 or 15 miles wide, on the Belgian mainland, which in its isolation may have been one of the loneliest and remotest parts of Europe. Yet it is only a few miles away from Bruges and Ghent and Antwerp. It has the old towns of Sluis and Hulst. But his journey's end was Axel, some five or six miles from the frontier with Belgium; and in view of what there is to tell it is interesting that Henri Havard states that the population of Axel, who are Protestants, are unmistakably Dutch in type, so that the foreigner feels he is still in Zeeland, while at Hulst, which is Catholic, both the population and the accent are Flemish. 'Never', he states, 'did two small towns present a more marked difference from each other,' yet they are only a quarter of an hour distant by train.

But indeed there was a particular reason for going to Axel, and it was under my persuasion that Mr Batsford undertook the journey. In fact, at Axel, the only interest is the local population. For the feminine costume, though dying out, is utterly and entirely fantastic; and what is more peculiar still, no drawing or photograph of this most medieval in appearance of all peasant dresses can be found before 1880, and it is the invention of the last decade or so of the nineteenth century. We would call this late flowering in a remote corner of Holland the last and ultimate fantasy of the kingdom of Cockaigne. For there can be no more. The peasant world is dead.

As could be expected Zeeusch-Vlanderen, to paraphrase Mr Batsford's account, shows landscapes more Flemish in feeling than Dutch – few canals, long lines of tall poplar trees contrasting with heathy stretches brilliant in spring with the gold of broom. Apart from the little border town of Hulst, where the old and once important fortified harbour held space for no fewer than 12 Spanish galleons in 1583, there is little else that calls for note. As for Axel, Mr Batsford dismisses it as one of the most unprepossessing towns in all Holland, a large proportion of its 7,000 inhabitants being engaged in a large saltpetre factory.

And now for the winged women of Axel, a dying race in 1947, if indeed any of them are now to be seen! They had, for it is wiser to speak in the past tense, peaked shoulders that were like a pair of wings. These rose above the level of the wearer's eyes, stiffened with canvas or paper, being really her fichu, and emerging from her waist. The *deuk* is the name for this pair of wings; and the other peculiarity of the Axel costume is the *beuk* or Zeeland chest-covering made here of pink and blue and other colours of beads sewn in beautiful and intricate patterns upon canvas, no two alike. In the colour plate in *The National Costumes of Holland* one girl wears a green flowered apron, and the other red. Their pairs of wings are of purple satin with a pattern of flowers in red and white and black, and of green satin with white and yellow flowers. The right-hand girl, over her red skirt, has a wide sash or bow of yellow broché with red and blue flowers upon it, and edged with fine gold lace. These ribbons, it is stated, were made in a variety of designs over a period of 40 years (at Coventry, one conjectures!) for this express purpose, and many of them had lovely designs, but even by 1932 they had largely disappeared.

Even the young girls were dressed in this manner. The smallest babes wore the Axel ribbon on their heads in black and red. Their pairs of wings would be of brown satin with blue and yellow flowers for working days; while their elders wore green satin wings with purple, green, black, red and yellow flowers. And their blue cotton aprons were curiously pleated into horizontal folds. The winged women were to be found nowhere else but between Axel and Terneuzen. In 1932 they still wore their beadwork breastplates, but their pairs of wings were of flowers and sprigs upon a black, and no longer a coloured ground. Inded, the 'angel' women would seem to belong more to the time of Geertzen tot Sint Jans, the Dutch primitive painter of the fifteenth century, than to the present. Their provenance is a mystery; but nothing is improbable in Holland which can be, at once, the most poetical and the most prosaic country in the world. It can be as odd or curious as Thailand or Korea; nowhere more so than with the 'angel' women of Axel, in this lonely, flat, and forgotten reach of the Dutch shore.

So ends the account of his excursion to Axel by Harry Batsford among the 'angel women', and I can see him in my mind's eye, half-stumbling, half-rushing along in his enthusiasm; one shoulder – always the left one – permanently weighed down by the accumulation of books, leaflets, postcards, chocolate, boiled sweets, and the unnecessary rubbish of all sorts and kinds carried round by him in his satchel. I shall always be grateful to him for taking me to Holland so soon after the War had ended. It was like a rejuvenation after the five long years of mental and visual incarceration.

When the first war ended, I had gone with my brother to Spain in April 1919 for a first experience of the Prado, the Escorial, and a week or more in Toledo. This second time of escapism the impression was of another nature altogether, but no less strong and no less lasting. It has been a delight to come back once more to the scene, and even be given the chance of enlarging it by going at long last to Zeeland. Veere and Zierickzee are an unspoilt delight, and not at all diminished in that sense in the long wait to see them; if much has gone in Zeeland, as in Friesland where not a single golden casque of the Frisian women was to be seen. But it remains Friesland all the same, and one would have it unaltered and no different.

Amsterdam might seem to the casual observer to have resisted change to a remarkable degree. This could be due to the unbelievable number of substantially built brick houses along both banks of its three main canals. And the old centre of The Hague stays unspoiled. Where else in Europe is there such a congeries of fine old houses! These confirm very closely to type and pattern; hence, the general, if now more and more disputed attribution of all and sundry to the Huguenot architect and general designer Daniel Marot. To this, the British Embassy at Westeinde 12 is an obvious exception, with character of its own and a hauntingly beautiful interior that once seen is not quickly forgotten.

In this present book, now reprinted after long interval, I tried to recapture the mood of the quiet and beautiful old Dutch buildings; and was no less delighted with the country Arcadias of the not-so-distant past. I do not think that anyone who has been to Hindeloopen – that dead town on the 'inland sea' of Holland with household arts of its own, but less than 900 inhabitants – or has climbed to the upper floor of the Frisian Museum at Leeuwarden and seen the fantastic and beautiful costumes – could dispute how I have written of them. But, rather, they explain the swarming, it had best be called, of good painters during the seventeenth century. The Hollanders produced three great geniuses in painting: Rembrandt, Vermeer, and at a later date, van Gogh. For the brilliant treatment of a foreshortened sleeve and hand, or the handling of the coloured sash of an inebriate arquebusier, and all in a bravura never before essayed on canvas, are not enough to put Franz Hals among the greatest artists there have ever been. But the sheer competence of such a number of good painters appearing without reason or explanation in the lifetime of two human generations, is an astonishment. And it remains so until you have seen what the Dutchmen could do with their lives in remote and unpromising surroundings. Then, it is no more a mystery. In comparison with most communities of human beings, ancient and modern, they led highly civilized lives. And perhaps the natural poetry that is lacking in their language was conveyed by them in compensation into the appurtenances of their daily lives. Those who would seek the truth of appearances must go to Holland for it is to be found there in Dutch painting.

What are no less conspicuous, though now fast fading, are the lesser lights and shadows from their golden age. To which extent this book reprinted has a happy content but must end a little sadly.

Index

Index